Nobel Lectures

# LITERATURE

2006 – 2010

# Nobel Lectures

Including Presentation Speeches and Laureates' Biographies

Physics

Chemistry

Physiology or Medicine

Literature

Economic Sciences

# NOBEL LECTURES

INCLUDING PRESENTATION SPEECHES AND LAUREATES' BIOGRAPHIES

# LITERATURE

## 2006 – 2010

EDITOR

**Per Wästberg**

The Swedish Academy, Stockholm, Sweden

World Scientific

NEW JERSEY • LONDON • SINGAPORE • BEIJING • SHANGHAI • HONG KONG • TAIPEI • CHENNAI

*Published by*

World Scientific Publishing Co. Pte. Ltd.
5 Toh Tuck Link, Singapore 596224
*USA office:* 27 Warren Street, Suite 401-402, Hackensack, NJ 07601
*UK office:* 57 Shelton Street, Covent Garden, London WC2H 9HE

**NOBEL LECTURES IN LITERATURE (2006–2010)**


Published with permission from Nobel Media AB in 2014 by World Scientific Publishing Co. Pte. Ltd.


ISBN 978-981-4583-11-4
ISBN 978-981-4583-12-1 (pbk)

Printed in Singapore by Mainland Press Pte Ltd.

# PREFACE

The Nobel Prize in Literature remains the most significant literary award in the world. After a shaky beginning, after some bad years in the 30s, it has, at least after 1945, some of the world's most influential and pathbreaking writers on its list. One must remember that a number of important authors, absent from that list, were never proposed or gained their reputation only posthumously.

With the Nobel Prize, Alfred Nobel — Europe's richest vagabond according to his friend Victor Hugo — created a cultural tradition that may become as durable as Dante and Shakespeare. Other prizes of even bigger monetary value have not managed to exceed the Nobel Prize in fame and importance.

In the Swedish Academy that nominates the five members of its Nobel Committee, we seek writers whose works have the force to open our eyes to unknown territories of the mind and have us witness realities that have eluded us. We navigate through the world, passing areas with unfruitful turbulence to enter zones not yet catalogued. We look for passages between different forms of identity, between various kinds of writing, always prepared to revise our mental map. There are no fixed norms, and the testament of Alfred Nobel allows all genres to be considered.

In the Swedish Academy, time and again, we hear from critics that first we should identify a place with a neglected language and, with the aid of experts, trace the most able representative of that area. Such a procedure, however, is bound to make the prize a political one. We do not allow a language, a nation, or sex and religion, ever to influence the choice of a writer whose individual originality and lifelong work we single out to the rest of the world's readers.

The present volume brings together the lectures, speeches and biographies for the period 2006–2010.

**Per Wästberg**
President of the Nobel Committee for Literature

# CONTENTS

Literature 2006

**Orhan Pamuk**

*"who in the quest for the melancholic soul of his native city has discovered new symbols for the clash and interlacing of cultures"*

# THE NOBEL PRIZE IN LITERATURE

Speech by Professor Horace Engdahl of the Swedish Academy.
Translation of the Swedish text.

Your Majesties, Your Royal Highnesses, Ladies and Gentlemen,

In his book about his native Istanbul, Orhan Pamuk describes how, as a young man, he was enraptured by a magnificent volume of early 19th-century engravings depicting the erstwhile capital of the vast Ottoman empire. The artist was German, embodying European landscape painting techniques and outlook – that combination of daydreaming and curiosity about the world that we call the picturesque and that was still alien to Turkish culture. But it was with genuine Istanbulite knowledge that the painter, after many years working in the city, saw the palaces, streets, throngs and the play of light on the Bosphorus waters. He had to be both Easterner – to understand what he was seeing – and Westerner to have the method to portray it.

Orhan Pamuk is describing here his own double view of reality. When Pamuk uses the Western form for the novel, it sheds its firm central perspective, tied to the protagonist's actions and emotions. Instead, we are drawn into a labyrinth of stories and beliefs, where the person we identify with can at any moment meet himself as a stranger, advancing from another direction, from another life or another culture.

In *My Name is Red*, Pamuk uses a sultan's painters of miniatures in 1590s Istanbul to stage a conflict between Western individualism and Eastern traditionalism. As the novel presents it, the classic Muslim standpoint is that paintings must illustrate familiar stories. To portray only what the eye sees in nature is a blasphemy. Ideally, one should paint from memory, painting the essence of the object and not its appearance, discarding everything extraneous and elevating oneself to Allah's view of the world. To leave traces in the work that can be identified as personal style was seen by the ancient masters as proof of ineptitude. For them, Western portraiture expressed a sinful desire to show pride before God. Anyone who would allow himself to be thus portrayed, believes himself to be singularly important and positions himself at the world's centre, as does the deliberately original artist with his style. Such a person will no longer bow to authorities but assumes the right to doubt everything and anything. That unique brushstroke, when the painter's hand obeys only his gaze, is a movement that threatens to topple every holy truth.

The choice between alternative views in the novel is seductively simple for a modern reader, but is revealed to be treacherous. At the same time as Pamuk, through his way of writing, appears to be on the side of personal style, he questions whether the unique stroke actually exists. Do not both love and art imply the imitation of gestures we have seen in others?

In Pamuk's major work, *The Black Book*, civilisation appears as a boundless plagiarism where people flee into each other's imagined lives to be free from themselves and experience love. You become what you describe. *The Black Book* is an odyssey through a night-time Istanbul full of genies and semi-beings, a city where invented stories attract more credibility than the true, and truth is a shadow on the wall. A dream world and a metaphor for the cosmos. Man's helpless need for narration has seldom been described more tellingly. Like Oscar Wilde pointing out that the Thames fog was imitating Turner's painting, Pamuk shows that the real Istanbul exists only because of its fabulists.

In his novel *Snow*, Pamuk travels to a forgotten town on a remote Turkish border. This displacement, no less drastic than a journey from Earth to Moon, gives him the opportunity to take a geological core sample of all levels of Turkish society, from the loyal state establishment to disappointed leftist intellectuals, Islamic fundamentalists, Kurds and the mystically suicidal girls fighting for the right to wear veils. In the centre of the story stands a Western-influenced poet looking for a way back from exile. *Snow* has been called a political novel, but more than the expression of an opinion, it is, like Dostoyevsky's *Demons*, a criticism of politics and its impact on the human mind. The fanatic's conviction stems from a blindness to the motivations of others. Against this, Pamuk puts the writer's emphatic identification with all his figures, beyond good and evil. The inherent irony of the events is the only judgment that he passes. The novel's charismatic fundamentalist, who terrifies the authorities and bewitches the woman the poet wants to love – on a mystic level, their struggle is Orpheus's defeat by Dionysus – this death-defying terrorist first of all strives to have his threats against Europe published in one of the big German newspapers so that the West will pay him notice. In the end, *Snow* is a book about the right to uncertainty and vacillation, about love as a lifelong defeat and about the longing for God.

Most honoured Orhan Pamuk,

You have made your native city an indispensable literary territory, equal to Dostoyevsky's St. Petersburg, Joyce's Dublin or Proust's Paris – a place where readers from all corners of the world can live another life, just as credible as their own, filled by an alien feeling that they immediately recognize as their own.

I would like to express the warm congratulations of the Swedish Academy as I now request you to receive this year's Nobel Prize for Literature from the hands of His Majesty the King.

# ORHAN PAMUK

Half of my book *Istanbul* is about the city; the other half chronicles the first 22 years of my life. I remember my huge disillusionment when it was finished. Of all the things I had wanted to express about my life, of all the memories that I considered the most crucial, only a few had found their way into the book. I could have written another twenty volumes describing the first twenty-two years of my life, each one drawing from a different set of experiences. It was then that I discovered that autobiographies served not to preserve our pasts, but to help us forget them.

I was born in Istanbul in 1952. My grandfather was a successful civil engineer and businessman who made his fortune building railroads and factories. My father followed in his footsteps, but instead of making money, he kept losing it. I was educated in private schools in Istanbul, and after studying architecture for three years, I dropped out, enrolled in a journalism course, and set out to become a writer. Between the ages of 7 and 22, I dreamed of being a painter. During my childhood and early youth, I painted with a happy and passionate sense of purpose. But by the time I stopped painting at the age of 22, I knew that I had no choice but to devote my life to art. At the same time, I had no idea why I gave up painting at the age of 22 and began to write my first novel, *Cevdet Bey and Sons*. It was to explore that mystery that, years later, I wrote *Istanbul.*

When I look back on my life up to the age of 54, I see a person who has worked long hours at a desk, in both happiness and in misery. I have written my books with care, patience, and good intentions, believing in each and every one. Success, fame, professional happiness... these did not come to me easily. Today my novels have been translated into 55 languages, but the hardest thing was finding a Turkish publisher for my first novel. It took me four years to find a publisher to take on *Cevdet Bey and Sons.* This despite the fact that it had won a national prize for unpublished novels...

In 1982 – at about the same time that I published my first novel, I married Aylin Türegün, and because we had both grown up in the same affluent, westernised Istanbul neighbourhood, walking the same streets and – before we ever knew each other – attending the same schools, I used to tease her by saying I had 'married a girl from my village'. Our daughter was born in 1991, and we named her after Rüya, the heroine of *The Black Book.*

I have made my living exclusively from writing. Between 1985 and 1988, I was a visiting scholar at Columbia University in New York, while my wife was working on her doctorate at the same university. I was greatly impressed by the richness of America's libraries, bookstores, and museums. My wife and I were divorced in 2002. She and our daughter remain my best friends. In 2006, a month before I won the Nobel Prize, I began to teach at Columbia University for one semester a year.

For me, a good day is a day like any other, when I have written one page well. Except for the hours I spend writing, life seems to me to be flawed, deficient, and senseless. Those who know me well understand how dependent I am on writing, tables, pens, and white paper, but they still urge me to 'take a bit of time off, do some travelling, enjoy life!' Those who know me even better understand that my greatest happiness is writing, so they tell me that nothing that keeps me far from writing, paper, and ink will ever do me any good. I am one of those rare happy creatures who have been able to do what they most desired, and who have been able to devote themselves to that task to the exclusion of all else.

I spent my childhood in a large family surrounded by uncles and aunts. My two first novels, *Cevdet Bey and Sons,* and *Silent House,* are family sagas. I enjoy describing crowded family gatherings – the meals they eat together, the feuds, and the quarrels. But with the passage of time, as our fortunes dwindled and our family dispersed, it gradually ceased to be a source of protection or a centre to which I felt obliged to return. Every night, when I curl up in bed and pull my quilt over me, I am swept away by a sweet fear that walks between solitude and dreams, the beauties of life, and its cruelties, and it is then that I shiver in the same way I did when I listened to scary stories, or read fairy tales, as a child.

In *Silent House,* it was through my grandmother's monologues that I tried to penetrate this world between sleep and wakefulness. There are traces of that same world in *The White Castle,* which also explores the shadows between dreams and reality, imagination and history. But it was in *The Black Book,* which I began in 1985, that I felt I found my own voice. I was 33 years old at the time, living in New York, and asking myself hard questions about who I was, and about my history. I spent all my time in my room in the Columbia Library, reading and writing. During my time in New York, my longing for Istanbul mixed in with my fascination for the wonders of Ottoman, Persian, Arab, and Islamic culture. *The Black Book* was a book that took me a very long time to plan, a book that I wrote without knowing exactly what I was doing, feeling my way forward like a blind man. I am still surprised that I was able to finish it.

*The New Life* is a lyrical exploration of the thing I first discovered in *The Black Book,* this time not in Istanbul, but in Anatolia. *My Name is Red* is the novel that perplexes my mother: she always tells me that she cannot understand how I wrote it... There is nothing in any of my other novels that surprises her; she knows that I drew upon the stuff of my own life. But in *My Name is Red* there is an aspect that she cannot connect with this son she knows so well, this son about whom she is certain that she knows everything... This must, in my view, be the greatest compliment to any writer can hear: to hear from his mother that his books are wiser than he is.

What has surprised me the most was the popularity of *Snow*. In the beginning I thought this was down to growing interest in political Islam, the clash of East-West stereotypes and their reflections in everyday life. But now I have come to think that what sets the book apart is what transpires in the *Hotel Asia* when the political activists are furiously preparing their statements. But in so thinking, I may have again misread my readers' minds. In the early nineties, when I was known only in Turkey, and Turkish journalists would sometimes ask me in a hostile way why people liked my books, and why I was so widely read, I'd come up with all sorts of reasons that I liked a great deal, but now I don't believe a single one of them. Later on, when I slowly came to be read all over the world, foreign journalists and literary critics began to ask the same question. I write the books I myself would like to read. And sometimes I take this to mean that everyone in the world shares my feelings. This attempt to explain the popularity of my books is probably as misguided as all the others. Even so, talking about one's books is as pointless as talking about one's life. In the end, a writer will see his life as more important than his books. But it is those books that give life its meaning and value. From the age of 22, when I began to write novels, I have never been able to separate my life from my novels. I think that the books I shall write in the future will be thought more entertaining, and more important, than my life. I take this to mean that a person must look ahead to the moment of his death, that he must resign himself to that moment. Despite this, it still seems that there is a lot of time left.

Because as I write these words at the age of 54 in April 2007, I know that my life has long since passed its midpoint, but, having written for thirty-two years now, I believe that I am at the midpoint of my career. I must have another thirty-two years in which to write more books, and to surprise my mother and other readers at least one more time.

*Translation from Turkish by Maureen Freely*

# MY FATHER'S SUITCASE

Nobel Lecture, December 7, 2006

by

ORHAN PAMUK

Istanbul, Turkey

Two years before his death, my father gave me a small suitcase filled with his writings, manuscripts and notebooks. Assuming his usual joking, mocking air, he told me he wanted me to read them after he was gone, by which he meant after he died.

'Just take a look,' he said, looking slightly embarrassed. 'See if there's anything inside that you can use. Maybe after I'm gone you can make a selection and publish it.'

We were in my study, surrounded by books. My father was searching for a place to set down the suitcase, wandering back and forth like a man who wished to rid himself of a painful burden. In the end, he deposited it quietly in an unobtrusive corner. It was a shaming moment that neither of us ever forgot, but once it had passed and we had gone back into our usual roles, taking life lightly, our joking, mocking personas took over and we relaxed. We talked as we always did, about the trivial things of everyday life, and Turkey's neverending political troubles, and my father's mostly failed business ventures, without feeling too much sorrow.

I remember that after my father left, I spent several days walking back and forth past the suitcase without once touching it. I was already familiar with this small, black, leather suitcase, and its lock, and its rounded corners. My father would take it with him on short trips and sometimes use it to carry documents to work. I remembered that when I was a child, and my father came home from a trip, I would open this little suitcase and rummage through his things, savouring the scent of cologne and foreign countries. This suitcase was a familiar friend, a powerful reminder of my childhood, my past, but now I couldn't even touch it. Why? No doubt it was because of the mysterious weight of its contents.

I am now going to speak of this weight's meaning. It is what a person creates when he shuts himself up in a room, sits down at a table, and retires to a corner to express his thoughts – that is, the meaning of literature.

When I did touch my father's suitcase, I still could not bring myself to open it, but I did know what was inside some of those notebooks. I had seen my father writing things in a few of them. This was not the first time I had heard of the heavy load inside the suitcase. My father had a large library; in his youth, in the late 1940s, he had wanted to be an Istanbul poet, and had translated Valéry into Turkish, but he had not wanted to live the sort of life that came with writing poetry in a poor country with few readers. My father's father – my grandfather – had been a wealthy business man; my father had led a comfortable life as a child and a young man, and he had no wish to endure hardship for the sake of literature, for writing. He loved life with all its beauties – this I understood.

The first thing that kept me distant from the contents of my father's suitcase was, of course, the fear that I might not like what I read. Because my father knew this, he had taken the precaution of acting as if he did not take its contents seriously. After working as a writer for 25 years, it pained me to see this. But I did not even want to be angry at my father for failing to take literature seriously enough… My real fear, the crucial thing that I did not wish to know or discover, was the possibility that my father might be a good writer. I couldn't open my father's suitcase because I feared this. Even worse, I couldn't even admit this myself openly. If true and great literature emerged from my father's suitcase, I would have to acknowledge that inside my father there existed an entirely different man. This was a frightening possibility. Because even at my advanced age I wanted my father to be only my father – not a writer.

A writer is someone who spends years patiently trying to discover the second being inside him, and the world that makes him who he is: when I speak of writing, what comes first to my mind is not a novel, a poem, or literary tradition, it is a person who shuts himself up in a room, sits down at a table, and alone, turns inward; amid its shadows, he builds a new world with words. This man – or this woman – may use a typewriter, profit from the ease of a computer, or write with a pen on paper, as I have done for 30 years. As he writes, he can drink tea or coffee, or smoke cigarettes. From time to time he may rise from his table to look out through the window at the children playing in the street, and, if he is lucky, at trees and a view, or he can gaze out at a black wall. He can write poems, plays, or novels, as I do. All these differences come after the crucial task of sitting down at the table and patiently turning inwards. To write is to turn this inward gaze into words, to study the world into which that person passes when he retires into himself, and to do so with patience, obstinacy, and joy. As I sit at my table, for days, months, years, slowly adding new words to the empty page, I feel as if I am creating a new world, as if I am bringing into being that other person inside me, in the same way someone might build a bridge or a dome, stone by stone. The stones we writers use are words. As we hold them in our hands, sensing the ways in which each of them is connected to the others, looking at them sometimes from afar, sometimes almost caressing them with our fingers and the tips of our pens, weighing them, moving them around, year in and year out, patiently and hopefully, we create new worlds.

The writer's secret is not inspiration – for it is never clear where it comes from – it is his stubbornness, his patience. That lovely Turkish saying – to dig a well with a needle – seems to me to have been said with writers in mind. In the old stories, I love the patience of Ferhat, who digs through mountains for his love – and I understand it, too. In my novel, *My Name is Red*, when I wrote about the old Persian miniaturists who had drawn the same horse with the same passion for so many years, memorising each stroke, that they could recreate that beautiful horse even with their eyes closed, I knew I was talking about the writing profession, and my own life. If a writer is to tell his own story – tell it slowly, and as if it were a story about other people – if he is to feel the power of the story rise up inside him, if he is to sit down at a table and patiently give himself over to this art – this craft – he must first have been given some hope. The angel of inspiration (who pays regular visits to some and rarely calls on others) favours the hopeful and the confident, and it is when a writer feels most lonely, when he feels most doubtful about his efforts, his dreams, and the value of his writing – when he thinks his story is only his story – it is at such moments that the angel chooses to reveal to him stories, images and dreams that will draw out the world he wishes to build. If I think back on the books to which I have devoted my entire life, I am most surprised by those moments when I have felt as if the sentences, dreams, and pages that have made me so ecstatically happy have not come from my own imagination – that another power has found them and generously presented them to me.

I was afraid of opening my father's suitcase and reading his notebooks because I knew that he would not tolerate the difficulties I had endured, that it was not solitude he loved but mixing with friends, crowds, salons, jokes, company. But later my thoughts took a different turn. These thoughts, these dreams of renunciation and patience, were prejudices I had derived from my own life and my own experience as a writer. There were plenty of brilliant writers who wrote surrounded by crowds and family life, in the glow of company and happy chatter. In addition, my father had, when we were young, tired of the monotony of family life, left us to go to Paris, where – like so many writers – he'd sat in his hotel room filling notebooks. I knew, too, that some of those very notebooks were in this suitcase, because during the years before he brought it to me, my father had finally begun to talk to me about that period in his life. He spoke about those years even when I was a child, but he would not mention his vulnerabilities, his dreams of becoming a writer, or the questions of identity that had plagued him in his hotel room. He would tell me instead about all the times he'd seen Sartre on the pavements of Paris, about the books he'd read and the films he'd seen, all with the elated sincerity of someone imparting very important news. When I became a writer, I never forgot that it was partly thanks to the fact that I had a father who would talk of world writers so much more than he spoke of pashas or great religious leaders. So perhaps I had to read my father's notebooks with this in mind, and remembering how indebted I was to his large library. I had to bear in mind that when he was living with us, my father, like me, enjoyed being alone with his books and his thoughts – and not pay too much attention to the literary quality of his writing.

But as I gazed so anxiously at the suitcase my father had bequeathed me, I also felt that this was the very thing I would not be able to do. My father would sometimes stretch out on the divan in front of his books, abandon the book in his hand, or the magazine and drift off into a dream, lose himself for the longest time in his thoughts. When I saw on his face an expression so very different from the one he wore amid the joking, teasing, and bickering of family life – when I saw the first signs of an inward gaze – I would, especially during my childhood and my early youth, understand, with trepidation, that he was discontent. Now, so many years later, I know that this discontent is the basic trait that turns a person into a writer. To become a writer, patience and toil are not enough: we must first feel compelled to escape crowds, company, the stuff of ordinary, everyday life, and shut ourselves up in a room. We wish for patience and hope so that we can create a deep world in our writing. But the desire to shut oneself up in a room is what pushes us into action. The precursor of this sort of independent writer – who reads his books to his heart's content, and who, by listening only to the voice of his own conscience, disputes with other's words, who, by entering into conversation with his books develops his own thoughts, and his own world – was most certainly Montaigne, in the earliest days of modern literature. Montaigne was a writer to whom my father returned often, a writer he recommended to me. I would like to see myself as belonging to the tradition of writers who – wherever they are in the world, in the East or in the West – cut themselves off from society, and shut themselves up with their books in their room. The starting point of true literature is the man who shuts himself up in his room with his books.

But once we shut ourselves away, we soon discover that we are not as alone as we thought. We are in the company of the words of those who came before us, of other people's stories, other people's books, other people's words, the thing we call tradition. I believe literature to be the most valuable hoard that humanity has gathered in its quest to understand itself. Societies, tribes, and peoples grow more intelligent, richer, and more advanced as they pay attention to the troubled words of their authors, and, as we all know, the burning of books and the denigration of writers are both signals that dark and improvident times are upon us. But literature is never just a national concern. The writer who shuts himself up in a room and first goes on a journey inside himself will, over the years, discover literature's eternal rule: he must have the artistry to tell his own stories as if they were other people's stories, and to tell other people's stories as if they were his own, for this is what literature is. But we must first travel through other people's stories and books.

My father had a good library – 1,500 volumes in all – more than enough for a writer. By the age of 22, I had perhaps not read them all, but I was familiar with each book – I knew which were important, which were light but easy to read, which were classics, which an essential part of any education, which were forgettable but amusing accounts of local history, and which French authors my father rated very highly. Sometimes I would look at this library from a distance and imagine that one day, in a different house, I would build my own library, an even better library – build myself a world. When I looked at my father's library from afar, it seemed to me to be a small picture of the real world. But this was a world seen from our own corner, from Istanbul.

The library was evidence of this. My father had built his library from his trips abroad, mostly with books from Paris and America, but also with books bought from the shops that sold books in foreign languages in the 40s and 50s and Istanbul's old and new booksellers, whom I also knew. My world is a mixture of the local – the national – and the West. In the 70s, I, too, began, somewhat ambitiously, to build my own library. I had not quite decided to become a writer – as I related in *Istanbul,* I had come to feel that I would not, after all, become a painter, but I was not sure what path my life would take. There was inside me a relentless curiosity, a hope-driven desire to read and learn, but at the same time I felt that my life was in some way lacking, that I would not be able to live like others. Part of this feeling was connected to what I felt when I gazed at my father's library – to be living far from the centre of things, as all of us who lived in Istanbul in those days were made to feel, that feeling of living in the provinces. There was another reason for feeling anxious and somehow lacking, for I knew only too well that I lived in a country that showed little interest in its artists – be they painters or writers – and that gave them no hope. In the 70s, when I would take the money my father gave me and greedily buy faded, dusty, dog-eared books from Istanbul's old booksellers, I would be as affected by the pitiable state of these second-hand bookstores – and by the despairing dishevelment of the poor, bedraggled booksellers who laid out their wares on roadsides, in mosque courtyards, and in the niches of crumbling walls – as I was by their books.

As for my place in the world – in life, as in literature, my basic feeling was that I was 'not in the centre'. In the centre of the world, there was a life richer and more exciting than our own, and with all of Istanbul, all of Turkey, I was outside it. Today I think that I share this feeling with most people in the world. In the same way, there was a world literature, and its centre, too, was very far away from me. Actually what I had in mind was Western, not world, literature, and we Turks were outside it. My father's library was evidence of this. At one end, there were Istanbul's books – our literature, our local world, in all its beloved detail – and at the other end were the books from this other, Western, world, to which our own bore no resemblance, to which our lack of resemblance gave us both pain and hope. To write, to read, was like leaving one world to find consolation in the other world's otherness, the strange and the wondrous. I felt that my father had read novels to escape his life and flee to the West – just as I would do later. Or it seemed to me that books in those days were things we picked up to escape our own culture, which we found so lacking. It wasn't just by reading that we left our Istanbul lives to travel West – it was by writing, too. To fill those notebooks of his, my father had gone to Paris, shut himself up in his room, and then brought his writings back to Turkey. As I gazed at my father's suitcase, it seemed to me that this was what was causing me disquiet. After working in a room for 25 years to survive as a writer in Turkey, it galled me to see my father hide his deep thoughts inside this suitcase, to act as if writing was work that had to be done in secret, far from the eyes of society, the state, the people. Perhaps this was the main reason why I felt angry at my father for not taking literature as seriously as I did.

Actually I was angry at my father because he had not led a life like mine, because he had never quarrelled with his life, and had spent his life happily laughing with his friends and his loved ones. But part of me knew that I could also say that I was not so much 'angry' as 'jealous', that the second word was more accurate, and this, too, made me uneasy. That would be when I would ask myself in my usual scornful, angry voice: 'What is happiness?' Was happiness thinking that I lived a deep life in that lonely room? Or was happiness leading a comfortable life in society, believing in the same things as everyone else, or acting as if you did? Was it happiness, or unhappiness, to go through life writing in secret, while seeming to be in harmony with all around one? But these were overly ill-tempered questions. Wherever had I got this idea that the measure of a good life was happiness? People, papers, everyone acted as if the most important measure of a life was happiness. Did this alone not suggest that it might be worth trying to find out if the exact opposite was true? After all, my father had run away from his family so many times – how well did I know him, and how well could I say I understood his disquiet?

So this was what was driving me when I first opened my father's suitcase. Did my father have a secret, an unhappiness in his life about which I knew nothing, something he could only endure by pouring it into his writing? As soon as I opened the suitcase, I recalled its scent of travel, recognised several notebooks, and noted that my father had shown them to me years earlier, but without dwelling on them very long. Most of the notebooks I now took into my hands he had filled when he had left us and gone to Paris as a young man. Whereas I, like so many writers I admired – writers whose biographies I had read – wished to know what my father had written, and what he had thought, when he was the age I was now. It did not take me long to realise that I would find nothing like that here. What caused me most disquiet was when, here and there in my father's notebooks, I came upon a writerly voice. This was not my father's voice, I told myself; it wasn't authentic, or at least it did not belong to the man I'd known as my father. Underneath my fear that my father might not have been my father when he wrote, was a deeper fear: the fear that deep inside I was not authentic, that I would find nothing good in my father's writing, this increased my fear of finding my father to have been overly influenced by other writers and plunged me into a despair that had afflicted me so badly when I was young, casting my life, my very being, my desire to write, and my work into question. During my first ten years as a writer, I felt these anxieties more deeply, and even as I fought them off, I would sometimes fear that one day, I would have to admit to defeat – just as I had done with painting – and succumbing to disquiet, give up novel writing, too.

I have already mentioned the two essential feelings that rose up in me as I closed my father's suitcase and put it away: the sense of being marooned in the provinces, and the fear that I lacked authenticity. This was certainly not the first time they had made themselves felt. For years I had, in my reading and my writing, been studying, discovering, deepening these emotions, in all their variety and unintended consequences, their nerve endings, their triggers, and their many colours. Certainly my spirits had been jarred by the confusions, the sensitivities and the fleeting pains that life and books had sprung on me, most often as a young man. But it was only by writing books that I came to a fuller understanding of the problems of authenticity (as in *My Name is Red* and *The Black Book*) and the problems of life on the periphery (as in *Snow* and *Istanbul*). For me, to be a writer is to acknowledge the secret wounds that we carry inside us, the wounds so secret that we ourselves are barely aware of them, and to patiently explore them, know them, illuminate them, to own these pains and wounds, and to make them a conscious part of our spirits and our writing.

A writer talks of things that everyone knows but does not know they know. To explore this knowledge, and to watch it grow, is a pleasurable thing; the reader is visiting a world at once familiar and miraculous. When a writer shuts himself up in a room for years on end to hone his craft – to create a world – if he uses his secret wounds as his starting point, he is, whether he knows it or not, putting a great faith in humanity. My confidence comes from the belief that all human beings resemble each other, that others carry wounds like mine – that they will therefore understand. All true literature rises from this childish, hopeful certainty that all people resemble each other. When a writer shuts himself up in a room for years on end, with this gesture he suggests a single humanity, a world without a centre.

But as can be seen from my father's suitcase and the pale colours of our lives in Istanbul, the world did have a centre, and it was far away from us. In my books I have described in some detail how this basic fact evoked a Checkovian sense of provinciality, and how, by another route, it led to my questioning my authenticity. I know from experience that the great majority of people on this earth live with these same feelings, and that many suffer from an even deeper sense of insufficiency, lack of security and sense of degradation, than I do. Yes, the greatest dilemmas facing humanity are still landlessness, homelessness, and hunger… But today our televisions and newspapers tell us about these fundamental problems more quickly and more simply than literature can ever do. What literature needs most to tell and investigate today are humanity's basic fears: the fear of being left outside, and the fear of counting for nothing, and the feelings of worthlessness that come with such fears; the collective humiliations, vulnerabilities, slights, grievances, sensitivities, and imagined insults, and the nationalist boasts and inflations that are their next of kind… Whenever I am confronted by such sentiments, and by the irrational, overstated language in which they are usually expressed, I know they touch on a darkness inside me. We have often witnessed peoples, societies and nations outside the Western world – and I can identify with them easily – succumbing to fears that sometimes lead them to commit stupidities, all because of their fears of humiliation and their sensitivities. I also know that in the West – a world with which I can identify with the same ease – nations and peoples taking an excessive pride in their wealth, and in their having brought us the Renaissance, the Enlightenment, and Modernism, have, from time to time, succumbed to a self-satisfaction that is almost as stupid.

This means that my father was not the only one, that we all give too much importance to the idea of a world with a centre. Whereas the thing that compels us to shut ourselves up to write in our rooms for years on end is a faith in the opposite; the belief that one day our writings will be read and understood, because people all the world over resemble each other. But this, as I know from my own and my father's writing, is a troubled optimism, scarred by the anger of being consigned to the margins, of being left outside. The love and hate that Dostoyevsky felt towards the West all his life – I have felt this too, on many occasions. But if I have grasped an essential truth, if I have cause for optimism, it is because I have travelled with this great writer through his love-hate relationship with the West, to behold the other world he has built on the other side.

All writers who have devoted their lives to this task know this reality: whatever our original purpose, the world that we create after years and years of hopeful writing, will, in the end, move to other very different places. It will take us far away from the table at which we have worked with sadness or anger, take us to the other side of that sadness and anger, into another world. Could my father have not reached such a world himself? Like the land that slowly begins to take shape, slowly rising from the mist in all its colours like an island after a long sea journey, this other world enchants us. We are as beguiled as the western travellers who voyaged from the south to behold Istanbul rising from the mist. At the end of a journey begun in hope and curiosity, there lies before them a city of mosques and minarets, a medley of houses, streets, hills, bridges, and slopes, an entire world. Seeing it, we wish to enter into this world and lose ourselves inside it, just as we might with a book. After sitting down at a table because we felt provincial, excluded, on the margins, angry, or deeply melancholic, we have found an entire world beyond these sentiments.

What I feel now is the opposite of what I felt as a child and a young man: for me the centre of the world is Istanbul. This is not just because I have lived there all my life, but because, for the last 33 years, I have been narrating its streets, its bridges, its people, its dogs, its houses, its mosques, its fountains, its strange heroes, its shops, its famous characters, its dark spots, its days and its nights, making them part of me, embracing them all. A point arrived when this world I had made with my own hands, this world that existed only in my head, was more real to me than the city in which I actually lived. That was when all these people and streets, objects and buildings would seem to begin to talk amongst themselves, and begin to interact in ways I had not anticipated, as if they lived not just in my imagination or my books, but for themselves. This world that I had created like a man digging a well with a needle would then seem truer than all else.

My father might also have discovered this kind of happiness during the years he spent writing, I thought as I gazed at my father's suitcase: I should not prejudge him. I was so grateful to him, after all: he'd never been a commanding, forbidding, overpowering, punishing, ordinary father, but a father who always left me free, always showed me the utmost respect. I had often thought that if I had, from time to time, been able to draw from my imagination, be it in freedom or childishness, it was because, unlike so many of my friends from childhood and youth, I had no fear of my father, and I had sometimes believed very deeply that I had been able to become a writer because my father had, in his youth, wished to be one, too. I had to read him with tolerance – seek to understand what he had written in those hotel rooms.

It was with these hopeful thoughts that I walked over to the suitcase, which was still sitting where my father had left it; using all my willpower, I read through a few manuscripts and notebooks. What had my father written about? I recall a few views from the windows of Parisian hotels, a few poems, paradoxes, analyses… As I write I feel like someone who has just been in a traffic accident and is struggling to remember how it happened, while at the same time dreading the prospect of remembering too much. When I was a child, and my father and mother were on the brink of a quarrel – when they fell into one of those deadly silences – my father would at once turn on the radio, to change the mood, and the music would help us forget it all faster.

Let me change the mood with a few sweet words that will, I hope, serve as well as that music. As you know, the question we writers are asked most often, the favourite question, is; why do you write? I write because I have an innate need to write! I write because I can't do normal work like other people. I write because I want to read books like the ones I write. I write because I am angry at all of you, angry at everyone. I write because I love sitting in a room all day writing. I write because I can only partake in real life by changing it. I write because I want others, all of us, the whole world, to know what sort of life we lived, and continue to live, in Istanbul, in Turkey. I write because I love the smell of paper, pen, and ink. I write because I believe in literature, in the art of the novel, more than I believe in anything else. I write because it is a habit, a passion. I write because I am afraid of being forgotten. I write because I like the glory and interest that writing brings. I write to be alone. Perhaps I write because I hope to understand why I am so very, very angry at all of you, so very, very angry at everyone. I write because I like to be read. I write because once I have begun a novel, an essay, a page, I want to finish it. I write because everyone expects me to write. I write because I have a childish belief in the immortality of libraries, and in the way my books sit on the shelf. I write because it is exciting to turn all of life's beauties and riches into words. I write not to tell a story, but to compose a story. I write because I wish to escape from the foreboding that there is a place I must go but – just as in a dream – I can't quite get there. I write because I have never managed to be happy. I write to be happy.

A week after he came to my office and left me his suitcase, my father came to pay me another visit; as always, he brought me a bar of chocolate (he had forgotten I was 48 years old). As always, we chatted and laughed about life, politics and family gossip. A moment arrived when my father's eyes went to the corner where he had left his suitcase and saw that I had moved it. We looked each other in the eye. There followed a pressing silence. I did not tell him that I had opened the suitcase and tried to read its contents; instead I looked away. But he understood. Just as I understood that he had understood. Just as he understood that I had understood that he had understood. But all this understanding only went so far as it can go in a few seconds. Because my father was a happy, easygoing man who had faith in himself: he smiled at me the way he always did. And as he left the house, he repeated all the lovely and encouraging things that he always said to me, like a father.

As always, I watched him leave, envying his happiness, his carefree and unflappable temperament. But I remember that on that day there was also a flash of joy inside me that made me ashamed. It was prompted by the thought that maybe I wasn't as comfortable in life as he was, maybe I had not led as happy or footloose a life as he had, but that I had devoted it to writing – you've understood... I was ashamed to be thinking such things at my father's expense. Of all people, my father, who had never been the source of my pain – who had left me free. All this should remind us that writing and literature are intimately linked to a lack at the centre of our lives, and to our feelings of happiness and guilt.

But my story has a symmetry that immediately reminded me of something else that day, and that brought me an even deeper sense of guilt. Twenty-three years before my father left me his suitcase, and four years after I had decided, aged 22, to become a novelist, and, abandoning all else, shut myself up in a room, I finished my first novel, *Cevdet Bey and Sons;* with trembling hands I had given my father a typescript of the still unpublished novel, so that he could read it and tell me what he thought. This was not simply because I had confidence in his taste and his intellect: his opinion was very important to me because he, unlike my mother, had not opposed my wish to become a writer. At that point, my father was not with us, but far away. I waited impatiently for his return. When he arrived two weeks later, I ran to open the door. My father said nothing, but he at once threw his arms around me in a way that told me he had liked it very much. For a while, we were plunged into the sort of awkward silence that so often accompanies moments of great emotion. Then, when we had calmed down and begun to talk, my father resorted to highly charged and exaggerated language to express his confidence in me or my first novel: he told me that one day I would win the prize that I am here to receive with such great happiness.

He said this not because he was trying to convince me of his good opinion, or to set this prize as a goal; he said it like a Turkish father, giving support to his son, encouraging him by saying, 'One day you'll become a pasha!' For years, whenever he saw me, he would encourage me with the same words.

My father died in December 2002.

Today, as I stand before the Swedish Academy and the distinguished members who have awarded me this great prize – this great honour – and their distinguished guests, I dearly wish he could be amongst us.

*Translation from Turkish by Maureen Freely*

Portrait photo of Orhan Pamuk by photographer Ulla Montan.

Literature 2007

**Doris Lessing**

*"that epicist of the female experience, who with scepticism, fire and visionary power has subjected a divided civilisation to scrutiny"*

# THE NOBEL PRIZE IN LITERATURE

Speech by Writer Per Wästberg of the Swedish Academy.
Translation of the Swedish text.

Your Majesties, Your Royal Highnesses, Esteemed Nobel Laureates, Ladies and Gentlemen,

Doris Lessing is part of both the history of literature and living literature. She has contributed to changing the way we see the world. In all probability, no other Laureate has accumulated such a volume of work. We stroll through the great library of her work, where all sections are unmarked and all genre classification pointless. There is life and movement behind the broad or narrow spines of the books, resisting categorisation and the imposition of order.

Lessing links to the great narrative tradition of the 19th century but equally we may use her works as textbooks in 20th-century behavioural patterns, not least to discover the way many thought – or thought wrongly – during one of history's most turbulent periods as war succeeded war, colonialism was unmasked and communism in Europe conquered.

She has revealed the totalitarian temptations and shown us the strength of undogmatic humanism. She has displayed an almost limitless empathy with odd lives and a freedom from prejudice regarding every form of human behaviour. She was early in flagging global environmental threats and poverty and corruption in the Third World. She has given voice to the silent and to the refugees and homeless of our century – from Afghanistan to Zimbabwe. And as few others have done, she personified the woman's role in the 20th century.

She makes us exclaim: "How could she know?" since she was often first to speak about what no one else did. For her, nothing was too unimportant or insignificant. Which is why she batters at our hearts. But although she resembles a continent that initially defies exploration, she has never subscribed to the idea that the world is too complicated for clarification.

Undeterred, she peers under mossy stones and mouldy linoleum flooring, shying from nothing, and therefore becoming help and support for innumerable people. Like Frances in *The Sweetest Dream,* she takes care of everyone, a hospitable earth mother – later compiling perspicacious case studies of her visitors.

Doris Lessing writes as she breathes – to approach closer the trials and revelations of our existence. Eschewing protective gloves, she grasps our reality like a grubby root vegetable, uncovering experiences we did not realise we could access. Via thousands of intimate details and in lower-case letters – dare we call them feminine? – she phrases the eternal questions of how and why we live.

Her autobiographical novels were succeeded by memoirs from Rhodesia and London: *Under My Skin* and *Walking in the Shade.* They vibrate with sensuous life and manage unusually sharp focus in a telescopic rearview mirror, pitilessly probing social critique and a fearless ability to look inward. Lessing struggles with her parents, especially her mother, up to an advanced age, providing us with merciless images of motherhood. From the beginning, ideas, movements and feelings were swirling through the girl, making her a relentless witness of her time, and an authority-antagonist for whom the emperor is always naked.

*Walking in the Shade* ends in 1962 when *The Golden Notebook* became an epiphany for an entire generation of women. In this, Lessing's most experimental novel, battle is joined between the will to create and the desire to love. Obstacles are mapped for a woman seeking both independence and intimacy, since her freedom is paradoxically incomplete without the love that in turn undermines it. Lessing shows how conventions and other pitfalls along the way impede sensitive and passionate women from living authentically and fully, from glimpsing into the fifth, golden notebook.

Emotions blind and lead astray Lessing's heroines and endanger their free will. *Children of Violence* is the collective name for the five books about Martha Quest, Lessing's alter ego, who, in moving from a colonial existence to the British class hierarchy, is swept away by her dreams and primary instincts.

Chiefly female readers identified with Martha Quest's longing for freedom and disgust at hypocrisy and mendacity. A poor person in a rich society, a woman among men, a white among blacks, Doris Lessing worked to become the independent intellectual she was. She unveils the temptation of devotion to a utopia and absorption in a collective, and she illustrates how a triumphant ideology can deceive us with false redemption. She became a cartographer of disillusionment, drawing dystopias and catastrophes with frightening clarity.

Lessing has the ability to freely move into and away from herself, to barge in and become an invisible lodger. She often begins by observing her characters from within and then moving outside them, to strip them of their illusions from an objective distance. We can follow this eerie process in *The Summer before the Dark;* in the allegorical psycho-thriller about a monster child, *The Fifth Child;* and in *The Good Terrorist,* an in-depth account of the extreme leftwing squatting culture that sponges off female self-sacrifice.

In her later works, Lessing demolishes a long list of basic values. Left are the networks of family and friends, cats of course, and the foremothers and midwives in every sense who take responsibility, and always too much responsibility. And in this year's novel, *The Cleft,* she accords us a parable from the dawn of mankind – before the invention of love. Which is where she seems happiest, among hunters and gatherers, far from a contemporary culture that presages disorder and collapse.

Doris Lessing's epic landscapes shift from honest realism to symbolic fable, from the psychology of self-realisation to saga and myth. Using the lens of intuition, she has charted the changes from the decline of the empire through to a future earth ravaged by atomic warfare. Mara and Dann in the eco-fable of the same name flee from a new Ice Age to an uncertain foothold in what used to be Africa. In her massive *Canopus in Argos* suite she lets observers from another solar system report on our civilisation's ultimate phase. She moves freely across the plains of fantasy without raising her voice; she declines the rhetoric of doomsday preachers.

Ever since her African debut in 1950 with the tragic novel *The Grass Is Singing*, Lessing has disregarded boundaries: moral, gender or of habit. Solitude and social ostracism remain her thematic glue.

But when she occasionally draws a parallel between love and politics, it is because both stand for the hope we must try to sustain if living is to be worthwhile.

Dear Doris Lessing,

Age is no issue in literature. You are forever young and wise, old and rebellious. You are the least ingratiating of novelists. Your bout with destiny and reality is heavyweight-class; nothing has induced you to leave the ring. Throughout the world over the last 58 years, people have been warmed, provoked and led hand-in-hand by your books. You have helped us cope with some of our time's important concerns and you have created a document for the future to carry forward the flavour of an age, its prejudices and survival strategies, its everyday trifles and delights.

Your lifework and your great pioneering effort are today not fulfilled but crowned with a prize you have long deserved. The Swedish Academy sends you its warmest congratulations.

# DORIS LESSING

From the old stone house where I was born were views of the mountains with snow on them, and of the dusty plains that surround the little town. A high dry place. My mother said that the washing, put out to dry at eight in the morning was dry long before lunchtime. The outside world was present inside the house itself, in the person of a young American sharing the house with us. He was an oil man. "There were a lot of oil men around then". Thus did the future announce itself. It was his voice I remember but overlaid by probably a hundred American voices since.

It was 1919 when I was born. Many decades later a book came into my hands of the kind you see on "remaindered" boxes, or – once – second hand bookshops. It was written by a British "businessman", obviously an agent, or spy of some kind. He was ambling through Persia, through tribes and villages, sheep and shepherds. Long ago did this Persia disappear. He thoroughly enjoyed it all, and they were fascinated by him, this exotic from the outside world, and he was so interested in them, asking so many questions. He wrote about Kermanshah, where he said, the 1918–1919 flu epidemic took its toll. And the war had blown through there too. My parents had plentiful reminisces about those two years in Kermanshah, but nothing was said about the flu or the refugees from war.

There is one memory, indubitably from that time. My father rode to work at the bank, (The Imperial Bank of Persia) on a horse. Every morning I was lifted up, grasped by my father's hands on my ribs, to be put before him. I rode with him a short way, before he turned off onto a big road. Now, all that I remember is strong, even violent. First of all, the smell of horse, and then the slippery heat of the horse's hide under my palms. The heat of the horse on my legs. My father had his arm around me, and I leaned back into him. The smell of his jacket, the faintly smoky smell of tweed. And inside the tweed, the straps that went across his body and over his shoulder, to hold the wooden leg in position. The leg, responded with a hollow *knock* if you kicked it, was a legacy from the war – the Trenches.

When you see some little sprite of a girl or a little boy absorbed in his toy, you are seeing beings assaulted by storms of sensory inputs. In front of my father, I held tight – "Hold her tight, don't let her fall" – various female voices, irritants in this storm of smells, noises, sounds. We were going slowly towards the big gates, the horse moving awkwardly under me, my father's wooden leg straps poking into my back. The moment I was set down from the horse, I knew my father would set off on a trot and then a gallop. How I longed to be there still. But no. It was a slow walk, and my father's voice, just behind me, cajoled the horse, "Gently there, slow there..."

And as for what the little child you see there eats... Unless some late reversal of your taste buds allows you, every adult forgets what it is a small child tastes, what it has in its mouth – explosions of taste.

If I want to know what some small child is experiencing, I make myself remember that slow ride on my father's horse, gripped tight by my father. The smell of horse in itself is a giddying intoxicant.

Some memories have to be cherished, held tight, kept as reminders.

That was my best memory of my first two years, that and the smell that comes back at the words *market, bazaar,* a warm spicy smell, and the cries and commands in the other language.

And then there was Tehran, and I have so many memories, but one chief one, which is the birth of my brother.

No doubt this is a real memory, because everything is high around me, the loo handle miles above my head, my father who is ill, in a version of *couvade,* is on a high bed and I can scarcely see him. I am touching the frills of a cot, by reaching up my hand to them. My mother, tall and powerful, is standing by the cot with a baby, and urging me, saying "And this is your baby" and "Now you must love it." Well, it was not my baby, but I did indeed love it. This little scene was a motivator for the rest of my emotional life. Not till I wrote, late in my life, Mara and Dann, about how a small girl loves and guards her small brother, did I remember just how powerful was that injunction. "And now you must love him." But the lie there, "This is your baby," well, I never forgot that. Mistrust of bad faith, Trust once lost is not easily regained.

The three years in Tehran are a gallery of memories, but I will use three.

The little children are carried out to see the full moon, the stars. I lisped out the words for moon, stars, doubtless a dear little thing, but later when I was a horrible teenager, under another sky, other moons and stars, my father barked at me, "You were such lovely little things, with your 'mun, mun,' your 'stars,' but look at you now, who would believe you were ever such a pretty little thing." I did see his point, yes, and I did leave home about then, fifteen or so, I was.

If the moon and the stars were what every proud parent wants to show his little children, the next memory is fit for a treatise on nursery psychology. We are in the nursery in Tehran, I and my brother, undressing for bed, and I say to him, "What's that you've got there." And I point at his male equipment. Yet I have been familiar with my brother's sexual endowment for years, since he was born in fact. Yet, it seems, I only now notice it. "What's that you've got there?" And my brother, aged three, perhaps, four, pushes out his front, and points it at me. "Mine" he says, "it's mine." "My pee place is better that your pee place," I claim, vainly trying to make something impressive of my cleft. "It's mine, mine" said Harry, making of his penis a little bow, which he releases, at me. "You haven't got anything," he asserts. This scene I put into my novel *The Cleft,* as a key moment in the lives of those two little children. And of course we have all witnessed something similar if we have had any connection at all with nursery life. Surely a scene that must recur again and again, an exemplary Scene.

Then, from many memories one that is fit for the educationalists. It is winter, my mother has made a cat in snow, much more than life-size. It sits on its base of a box, draped in cloth, where snow is making patterns. The cat is sitting with its fore paws down, and it is looking out from green shiny eyes, a potent figure in the falling snow.

I am entranced, bewitched by this white cat. His eyes follow me, I cry "Look he is looking at me." And the cat does look, through the falling snow, which glitters. "Don't be silly" says my mother, "It's only bits of green stone." And she whisks out the cats eyes, one, two, shows me the bright green pebbles – and puts them back in.

Somewhere in a Tehran garden are lying two green pebbles, that were once a white cat's eyes, shining through falling snow.

Other memories – oh many, but then I am getting on for five, and the family is leaving Tehran, and we are going to get to England via Moscow. There is a train from the Caspian to Moscow. For those Edwardians, my parents, a train means dining cars and conductors, something safe and regulated, not dangerous, for my mother wasn't going to take her precious little children through the Red Sea in all that heat.

And now the memories are a river, a flood. First that train journey through Russia, on a train recently a troop train, dirty, with torn seats, needing applications of insect powder. No food on the train. My mother leaped down at the stations to buy hardboiled eggs and pies from the peasant women. She was left behind on a station, and then, without a word of Russian, she stopped the next train, commandeered it and caught up with our train the next day: panic, even terror. Never will I forget those stations, each crowded with raggedy hungry children, who had lost parents in the Civil War. It was possible for children not to have a mother, a father? More panic. And each station crowded with people and children who saw our dilapidated train as a promise of food and safety. Then Moscow, a real hotel and then a boat through the Baltic States. Years later I was in Riga, saw the little park where I played with my brother but it had been war damaged (like Kermanshah in the Iran war, like Zimbabwe years later). And the hotel was there but are those memories really mine or clips from a Bergman film. His films love wide hotel corridors, not like nowadays, into which may come a dwarf, strolling players, a kind of old man beckoning one into amazing secrets…

England. I loathed it. Not a false memory. I had come from high, dry sunlit Persia where there was snow on the mountains. And now – one memory sums it all up. A fishmonger's slab, with its dead staring fish, and over them weakly clambers a black lobster, "looking for the sea" someone says, "Yes, it's not going to find the sea again," and the grey rain falling – six months of England.

The boat, the sea voyage. My mother liked the captain, and they had jolly times, while poor father, very sea sick, lay on his bunk.

At evening they danced and dined, and I wanting to join in was told that I wouldn't enjoy it. Of course I would enjoy it. I behaved badly to punish my mother for her lie. I tried to cut up her evening dresses with a little pair of nail scissors. I went on behaving badly during a journey lit with marvels... "Look at that, look at the ostriches!" There they were, highstepping it across some sandy flat, and then after so much wicked behaviour on my part, and I was on the wagon (a covered wagon, like on the films) where I lay at night and watched the hurricane lamp swaying where it hung from the canvas, and beyond that the bush and the noises of the night.

What about that house, the building of it... It was very quick, building that house. You dig a trench, insert poles cut from the bush, tie them with the wonderfully smelling apricot coloured "bush rope," the fleshy underbark of the Mususa tree, you slap handfuls of mud on to the poles, cover it all with sheaves of fragrant new cut grass, doors and windows appear, and there is the house, which soon we occupied.

Of course there were minor setbacks, like all the family getting married, not once, but twice.

I could rhapsodise, which I tend to do, secretly, remembering prize moments, about the warm glow of the oil lamps on the white shed walls, and the gleaming thatch.

But now I suppose must begin that adventure which was my life, shall I dwell on the horrors of the convent school, where I was so unhappy, nothing in my life could ever be as bad.

Much better the times in the bush, where I was so often, by myself or with my brother.

The point of these memories is that they are beyond reach, now for as far away as "Scenes from the Boer War" might be for my parents. It was virgin bush, our farm, full of the animals born to be there. The elephants had gone, and the lions, but all the rest were there, and wandering out in the early morning just down the hill a few paces, I might see Kudu, the eland, the little duiker, a porcupine, snakes, the little bush monkeys some people made into pets and which might flit across the rafters of our house at night.

I would stand outside my room and look down on the backs of hunting hawks, as they soared over the maize fields.

These animals are in game parks now.

The birds are always fewer and fewer. Whites and blacks, are too much for the animals and birds who once said "This bush is ours..."

There were a hundred adventures and pleasures in the bush.

And now I must record that my brother and I became friends late in life and I would reminisce about my days in the bush, but noticed he was often silent.

He said he did not remember anything at all before he was eleven. "What, nothing?"

Nothing.

"You don't remember how we were in the bush and some wild pig chased us and we went up a tree and you were laughing so hard you nearly fell straight down in front of her?"

"No I don't remember."

"You don't remember how we walked to the river and sat and watched the troop of baboons feeding and drinking until the big baboon gesticulated and threatened us, until we gave in and went away?"

"No"

"You don't remember how we…"

"No, nothing"

There sat my brother across from me at the table, and my mind was full of memories, but his mind, he said was a blank.

*How was that possible?*

When he was seven, he said, he would take the cookboy's son with him, with a gun, and some bread, and go off into the bush for days.

"We had all kinds of jolly good chinwags, I can tell you."

Then I was in the city, for a year I was one of the girls. A small number of the city's eligible young men, and the girls – we went to the bioscope every night (the films) and wore evening dresses. The provinces tend to make great occasions out of the ordinary. We danced too. When I say "We" I mean the young whites.

And then there was the war, and I got married, because that is what happens in a war and for three years I was the most conventional white madam, doing everything just right, cooking, making clothes and there were two babes. How infinitely adaptable we all are. I hated the life, the society – one hundred thousand whites commanded half a million blacks in old Southern Rhodesia.

I left that marriage, married a German refugee, Gottfried Lessing, had another child. Having babies when you are very young is really very easy: it seems one must make this point now, when getting children seems to be increasingly difficult.

Ten years of the war. The colony was full of the refugees from Europe and then the RAF. Amazing that this chapter of the war should be forgotten.

1939 to 1945. From '45 to '49 were the worst years of my life. I longed to leave for England, which is where I would have gone in '38, '39 if I had had the money. I couldn't leave at once then, because of complications over Gottfried wanting to get British nationality: a divorce would not have helped him. But I stuck it out and we got amicably divorced and at last I did leave for England. I think all the rest has been adequately chronicled.

I felt as if my real life was beginning when I at last arrived in war-torn, grubby, cold England. And of course, it was. Since then, I have written, that has been my life.

Very hard work, life is – that's my summing up as I reach the end of life. "Oh such hard work. All of it."

For most of the time I had a child and we all know that the life of a writer is better without small children. But that is not to say I had ever wished the child away. And I even at various points in my life added children and young people when I didn't have to, as in *The Sweetest Dream*, for instance. But the real story of a life is in the record of the memories or dreams… and where should I begin, or end? Once I thought I would write my autobiography in dreams. My failed attempt became *Memoirs of a Survivor*. Dreams, a dream, have often rescued me when stuck in a story or a novel.

# ON NOT WINNING THE NOBEL PRIZE

Nobel Lecture, December 7, 2007

by

DORIS LESSING

24, Gondar Gardens, London NW6 1 HG, England.

I am standing in a doorway looking through clouds of blowing dust to where I am told there is still uncut forest. Yesterday I drove through miles of stumps, and charred remains of fires where, in '56, there was the most wonderful forest I have ever seen, all now destroyed. People have to eat. They have to get fuel for fires.

This is north-west Zimbabwe in the early eighties, and I am visiting a friend who was a teacher in a school in London. He is here "to help Africa," as we put it. He is a gently idealistic soul and what he found in this school shocked him into a depression, from which it was hard to recover. This school is like every other built after Independence. It consists of four large brick rooms side by side, put straight into the dust, one two three four, with a half room at one end, which is the library. In these classrooms are blackboards, but my friend keeps the chalks in his pocket, as otherwise they would be stolen. There is no atlas or globe in the school, no textbooks, no exercise books, or biros. In the library there are no books of the kind the pupils would like to read, but only tomes from American universities, hard even to lift, rejects from white libraries, or novels with titles like *Weekend in Paris* and *Felicity Finds Love.*

There is a goat trying to find sustenance in some aged grass. The headmaster has embezzled the school funds and is suspended, arousing the question familiar to all of us but usually in more august contexts: How is it these people behave like this when they must know everyone is watching them?

My friend doesn't have any money because everyone, pupils and teachers, borrow from him when he is paid and will probably never pay him back. The pupils range from six to twenty-six, because some who did not get schooling as children are here to make it up. Some pupils walk many miles every morning, rain or shine and across rivers. They cannot do homework because there is no electricity in the villages, and you can't study easily by the light of a burning log. The girls have to fetch water and cook before they set off for school and when they get back.

As I sit with my friend in his room, people drop in shyly, and everyone begs for books. "Please send us books when you get back to London," one man says. "They taught us to read but we have no books." Everybody I met, everyone, begged for books.

I was there some days. The dust blew. The pumps had broken and the women were having to fetch water from the river. Another idealistic teacher from England was rather ill after seeing what this "school" was like.

On the last day they slaughtered the goat. They cut it into bits and cooked it in a great tin. This was the much anticipated end-of-term feast: boiled goat and porridge. I drove away while it was still going on, back through the charred remains and stumps of the forest.

I do not think many of the pupils of this school will get prizes.

The next day I am to give a talk at a school in North London, a very good school, whose name we all know. It is a school for boys, with beautiful buildings and gardens.

These children here have a visit from some well known person every week, and it is in the nature of things that these may be fathers, relatives, even mothers of the pupils. A visit from a celebrity is not unusual for them.

As I talk to them, the school in the blowing dust of north-west Zimbabwe is in my mind, and I look at the mildly expectant English faces in front of me and try to tell them about what I have seen in the last week. Classrooms without books, without textbooks, or an atlas, or even a map pinned to a wall. A school where the teachers beg to be sent books to tell them how to teach, they being only eighteen or nineteen themselves. I tell these English boys how everybody begs for books: "Please send us books." I am sure that anyone who has ever given a speech will know that moment when the faces you are looking at are blank. Your listeners cannot hear what you are saying, there are no images in their minds to match what you are telling them – in this case the story of a school standing in dust clouds, where water is short, and where the end of term treat is a just-killed goat cooked in a great pot.

Is it really so impossible for these privileged students to imagine such bare poverty?

I do my best. They are polite.

I'm sure that some of them will one day win prizes.

Then, the talk is over. Afterwards I ask the teachers how the library is, and if the pupils read. In this privileged school, I hear what I always hear when I go to such schools and even universities.

"You know how it is," one of the teacher's says. "A lot of the boys have never read at all, and the library is only half used."

Yes, indeed we do know how it is. All of us.

We are in a fragmenting culture, where our certainties of even a few decades ago are questioned and where it is common for young men and women, who have had years of education, to know nothing of the world, to have read nothing, knowing only some speciality or other, for instance, computers.

What has happened to us is an amazing invention – computers and the internet and TV. It is a revolution. This is not the first revolution the human race has dealt with. The printing revolution, which did not take place in a matter of a few decades, but took much longer, transformed our minds and ways of thinking. A foolhardy lot, we accepted it all, as we always do, never asked, What is going to happen to us now, with this invention of print? In the same way, we never thought to ask, How will our lives, our way of thinking, be changed by this internet, which has seduced a whole generation with its inanities so that even quite reasonable people will confess that once they are hooked, it is hard to cut free, and they may find a whole day has passed in blogging etc.

Very recently, anyone even mildly educated would respect learning, education, and our great store of literature. Of course, we all know that when this happy state was with us, people would pretend to read, would pretend respect for learning. But it is on record that working men and women longed for books, and this is evidenced by the founding of working men's libraries and institutes, the colleges of the $18^{th}$ and $19^{th}$ centuries.

Reading, books, used to be part of a general education.

Older people, talking to young ones, must understand just how much of an education reading was, because the young ones know so much less. And if children cannot read, it is because they have not read.

We all know this sad story.

But we do not know the end of it.

We think of the old adage, "Reading maketh a full man" – and forgetting about jokes to do with over-eating – reading makes a woman and a man full of information, of history, of all kinds of knowledge.

But we in the West are not the only people in the world. Not long ago a friend who had been in Zimbabwe told me about a village where people had not eaten for three days, but they were still talking about books and how to get them, about education.

I belong to an organisation which started out with the intention of getting books into the villages. There was a group of people who in another connection had travelled Zimbabwe at its grass roots. They told me that the villages, unlike what is reported, are full of intelligent people, teachers retired, teachers on leave, children on holidays, old people. I myself paid for a little survey to discover what people in Zimbabwe want to read, and found the results were the same as those of a Swedish survey I had not known about. People want to read the same kinds of books that we in Europe want to read – novels of all kinds, science fiction, poetry, detective stories, plays, and do-it-yourself books, like how to open a bank account. All of Shakespeare too. A problem with finding books for villagers is that they don't know what is available, so a set book, like the *Mayor of Casterbridge,* becomes popular simply because it just happens to be there. *Animal Farm,* for obvious reasons, is the most popular of all novels.

Our organisation was helped from the very start by Norway, and then by Sweden. Without this kind of support our supplies of books would have dried up. We got books from wherever we could. Remember, a good paperback from England costs a month's wages in Zimbabwe: that was *before* Mugabe's reign of terror. Now with inflation, it would cost several years' wages. But having taken a box of books out to a village – and remember there is a terrible shortage of petrol – I can tell you that the box was greeted with tears. The library may be a plank on bricks under a tree. And within a week there will be literacy classes – people who can read teaching those who can't, citizenship classes – and in one remote village, since there were no novels written in the language Tonga, a couple of lads sat down to write novels in Tonga. There are six or so main languages in Zimbabwe and there are novels in all of them: violent, incestuous, full of crime and murder.

It is said that a people gets the government it deserves, but I do not think it is true of Zimbabwe. And we must remember that this respect and hunger for books comes, not from Mugabe's regime, but from the one before it, the whites. It is an astonishing phenomenon, this hunger for books, and it can be seen everywhere from Kenya down to the Cape of Good Hope.

This links improbably with a fact: I was brought up in what was virtually a mud hut, thatched. This kind of house has been built always, everywhere there are reeds or grass, suitable mud, poles for walls. Saxon England for example. The one I was brought up in had four rooms, one beside another, and it was full of books. Not only did my parents take books from England to Africa, but my mother ordered books by post from England for her children. Books arrived in great brown paper parcels, and they were the joy of my young life. A mud hut, but full of books.

Even today I get letters from people living in a village that might not have electricity or running water, just like our family in our elongated mud hut. "I shall be a writer too," they say, "because I've the same kind of house you lived in."

But here is the difficulty, no?

Writing, writers, do not come out of houses without books.

There is the gap. There is the difficulty.

I have been looking at the speeches by some of your recent prizewinners. Take the magnificent Pamuk. He said his father had 500 books. His talent did not come out of the air, he was connected with the great tradition.

Take V. S. Naipaul. He mentions that the Indian Vedas were close behind the memory of his family. His father encouraged him to write, and when he got to England he would visit the British Library. So he was close to the great tradition.

Let us take John Coetzee. He was not only close to the great tradition, he was the tradition: he taught literature in Cape Town. And how sorry I am that I was never in one of his classes, taught by that wonderfully brave, bold mind.

In order to write, in order to make literature, there must be a close connection with libraries, books, with the Tradition.

I have a friend from Zimbabwe, a Black writer. He taught himself to read from the labels on jam jars, the labels on preserved fruit cans. He was brought up in an area I have driven through, an area for rural blacks. The earth is grit and gravel, there are low sparse bushes. The huts are poor, nothing like the well cared-for huts of the better off. A school – but like one I have described. He found a discarded children's encyclopaedia on a rubbish heap and taught himself from that.

On Independence in 1980 there was a group of good writers in Zimbabwe, truly a nest of singing birds. They were bred in old Southern Rhodesia, under the whites – the mission schools, the better schools. Writers are not made in Zimbabwe. Not easily, not under Mugabe.

All the writers travelled a difficult road to literacy, let alone to becoming writers. I would say learning to read from the printed labels on jam jars and discarded encyclopaedias was not uncommon. And we are talking about people hungering for standards of education beyond them, living in huts with many children – an overworked mother, a fight for food and clothing.

Yet despite these difficulties, writers came into being. And we should also remember that this was Zimbabwe, conquered less than a hundred years before. The grandparents of these people might have been storytellers working in the oral tradition. In one or two generations there was the transition from stories remembered and passed on, to print, to books. What an achievement.

Books, literally wrested from rubbish heaps and the detritus of the white man's world. But a sheaf of paper is one thing, a published book quite another. I have had several accounts sent to me of the publishing scene in Africa. Even in more privileged places like North Africa, with its different tradition, to talk of a publishing scene is a dream of possibilities.

Here I am talking about books never written, writers that could not make it because the publishers are not there. Voices unheard. It is not possible to estimate this great waste of talent, of potential. But even before that stage of a book's creation which demands a publisher, an advance, encouragement, there is something else lacking.

Writers are often asked, How do you write? With a wordprocessor? an electric typewriter? a quill? longhand? But the essential question is, "Have you found a space, that empty space, which should surround you when you write?" Into that space, which is like a form of listening, of attention, will come the words, the words your characters will speak, ideas – inspiration.

If a writer cannot find this space, then poems and stories may be stillborn.

When writers talk to each other, what they discuss is always to do with this imaginative space, this other time. "Have you found it? Are you holding it fast?"

Let us now jump to an apparently very different scene. We are in London, one of the big cities. There is a new writer. We cynically enquire, Is she good-looking? If this is a man, charismatic? Handsome? We joke but it is not a joke.

This new find is acclaimed, possibly given a lot of money. The buzzing of paparazzi begins in their poor ears. They are feted, lauded, whisked about the world. Us old ones, who have seen it all, are sorry for this neophyte, who has no idea of what is really happening.

He, she, is flattered, pleased.

But ask in a year's time what he or she is thinking – I've heard them: "This is the worst thing that could have happened to me," they say.

Some much publicised new writers haven't written again, or haven't written what they wanted to, meant to.

And we, the old ones, want to whisper into those innocent ears. "Have you still got your space? Your soul, your own and necessary place where your own voices may speak to you, you alone, where you may dream. Oh, hold onto it, don't let it go."

My mind is full of splendid memories of Africa which I can revive and look at whenever I want. How about those sunsets, gold and purple and orange, spreading across the sky at evening. How about butterflies and moths and bees on the aromatic bushes of the Kalahari? Or, sitting on the pale grassy banks of the Zambesi, the water dark and glossy, with all the birds of Africa darting about. Yes, elephants, giraffes, lions and the rest, there were plenty of those, but how about the sky at night, still unpolluted, black and wonderful, full of restless stars.

There are other memories too. A young African man, eighteen perhaps, in tears, standing in what he hopes will be his "library." A visiting American seeing that his library had no books, had sent a crate of them. The young man had taken each one out, reverently, and wrapped them in plastic. "But," we say, "these books were sent to be read, surely?" "No," he replies, "they will get dirty, and where will I get any more?"

This young man wants us to send him books from England to use as teaching guides. "I only did four years in senior school," he says, "but they never taught me to teach."

I have seen a teacher in a school where there were no textbooks, not even a chalk for the blackboard. He taught his class of six to eighteen year olds by moving stones in the dust, chanting "Two times two is..." and so on. I have seen a girl, perhaps not more than twenty, also lacking textbooks, exercise books, biros, seen her teach the A B C by scratching the letters in the dirt with a stick, while the sun beat down and the dust swirled.

We are witnessing here that great hunger for education in Africa, anywhere in the Third World, or whatever we call parts of the world where parents long to get an education for their children which will take them out of poverty.

I would like you to imagine yourselves somewhere in Southern Africa, standing in an Indian store, in a poor area, in a time of bad drought. There is a line of people, mostly women, with every kind of container for water. This store gets a bowser of precious water every afternoon from the town, and here the people wait.

The Indian is standing with the heels of his hands pressed down on the counter, and he is watching a black woman, who is bending over a wadge of paper that looks as if it has been torn from a book. She is reading *Anna Karenin.*

She is reading slowly, mouthing the words. It looks a difficult book. This is a young woman with two little children clutching at her legs. She is pregnant. The Indian is distressed, because the young woman's headscarf, which should be white, is yellow with dust. Dust lies between her breasts and on her arms. This man is distressed because of the lines of people, all thirsty. He doesn't have enough water for them. He is angry because he knows there are people dying out there, beyond the dust clouds. His older brother had been here holding the fort, but he had said he needed a break, had gone into town, really rather ill, because of the drought.

This man is curious. He says to the young woman, "What are you reading?"

"It is about Russia," says the girl.

"Do you know where Russia is?" He hardly knows himself.

The young woman looks straight at him, full of dignity, though her eyes are red from dust, "I was best in the class. My teacher said I was best."

The young woman resumes her reading. She wants to get to the end of the paragraph.

The Indian looks at the two little children and reaches for some Fanta, but the mother says, "Fanta makes them thirstier."

The Indian knows he shouldn't do this but he reaches down to a great plastic container beside him, behind the counter, and pours out two mugs of water, which he hands to the children. He watches while the girl looks at her children drinking, her mouth moving. He gives her a mug of water. It hurts him to see her drinking it, so painfully thirsty is she.

Now she hands him her own plastic water container, which he fills. The young woman and the children watch him closely so that he doesn't spill any.

She is bending again over the book. She reads slowly. The paragraph fascinates her and she reads it again.

*"Varenka, with her white kerchief over her black hair, surrounded by the children and gaily and good-humouredly busy with them, and at the same visibly excited at the possibility of an offer of marriage from a man she cared for, looked very attractive. Koznyshev walked by her side and kept casting admiring glances at her. Looking at her, he recalled all the delightful things he had heard from her lips, all the good he knew about her, and became more and more conscious that the feeling he had for her was something rare, something he had felt but once before, long, long ago, in his early youth. The joy of being near her increased step by step, and at last reached such a point that, as he put a huge birch mushroom with a slender stalk and up-curling top into her basket, he looked into her eyes and, noting the flush of glad and frightened agitation that suffused her face, he was confused himself, and in silence gave her a smile that said too much."*

This lump of print is lying on the counter, together with some old copies of magazines, some pages of newspapers with pictures of girls in bikinis.

It is time for the woman to leave the haven of the Indian store, and set off back along the four miles to her village. Outside, the lines of waiting women clamour and complain. But still the Indian lingers. He knows what it will cost this girl – going back home, with the two clinging children. He would give her the piece of prose that so fascinates her, but he cannot really believe this splinter of a girl with her great belly can really understand it.

Why is perhaps a third of *Anna Karenin* here on this counter in a remote Indian store? It is like this.

A certain high official, from the United Nations as it happens, bought a copy of this novel in a bookshop before he set out on his journey to cross several oceans and seas. On the plane, settled in his business class seat, he tore the book into three parts. He looked around his fellow passengers as he did this, knowing he would see looks of shock, curiosity, but some of amusement. When he was settled, his seat belt tight, he said aloud to whomever could hear, "I always do this when I've a long trip. You don't want to have to hold up some heavy great book." The novel was a paperback, but, true, it is a long book. This man is well used to people listening when he spoke. "I always do this, travelling," he confided. "Travelling at all these days, is hard enough." And as soon as people were settling down, he opened his part of *Anna Karenin,* and read. When people looked his way, curiously or not, he confided in them. "No, it really is the only way to travel." He knew the novel, liked it, and this original mode of reading did add spice to what was after all a well known book.

When he reached the end of a section of the book, he called the air hostess, and sent the chapters back to his secretary, travelling in the cheaper seats. This caused much interest, condemnation, certainly curiosity, every time a section of the great Russian novel arrived, mutilated but readable, in the back part of the plane. Altogether, this clever way of reading Anna *Karenin* makes an impression, and probably no one there would forget it.

Meanwhile, in the Indian store, the young woman is holding on to the counter, her little children clinging to her skirts. She wears jeans, since she is a modern woman, but over them she has put on the heavy woollen skirt, part of the traditional dress of her people: her children can easily cling onto its thick folds.

She sends a thankful look to the Indian, whom she knew liked her and was sorry for her, and she steps out into the blowing clouds.

The children are past crying, and their throats are full of dust.

This was hard, oh yes, it was hard, this stepping, one foot after another, through the dust that lay in soft deceiving mounds under her feet. Hard, but she was used to hardship, was she not? Her mind was on the story she had been reading. She was thinking, She is just like me, in her white headscarf, and she is looking after children, too. I could be her, that Russian girl. And the man there, he loves her and will ask her to marry him. She had not finished more than that one paragraph. Yes, she thinks, a man will come for me, and take me away from all this, take me and the children, yes, he will love me and look after me.

She steps on. The can of water is heavy on her shoulders. On she goes. The children can hear the water slopping about. Half way she stops, sets down the can.

Her children are whimpering and touching it. She thinks that she cannot open it, because dust would blow in. There is no way she can open the can until she gets home.

"Wait," she tells her children, "wait."

She has to pull herself together and go on.

She thinks, My teacher said there is a library, bigger than the supermarket, a big building and it is full of books. The young woman is smiling as she moves on, the dust blowing in her face. I am clever, she thinks. Teacher said I am clever. The cleverest in the school – she said I was. My children will be clever, like me. I will take them to the library, the place full of books, and they will go to school, and they will be teachers – my teacher told me I could be a teacher. My children will live far from here, earning money. They will live near the big library and enjoy a good life.

You may ask how that piece of the Russian novel ever ended up on that counter in the Indian store?

It would make a pretty story. Perhaps someone will tell it.

On goes that poor girl, held upright by thoughts of the water she will give her children once home, and drink a little of herself. On she goes, through the dreaded dusts of an African drought.

We are a jaded lot, we in our threatened world. We are good for irony and even cynicism. Some words and ideas we hardly use, so worn out have they become. But we may want to restore some words that have lost their potency.

We have a treasure-house of literature, going back to the Egyptians, the Greeks, the Romans. It is all there, this wealth of literature, to be discovered again and again by whoever is lucky enough to come upon it. A treasure. Suppose it did not exist. How impoverished, how empty we would be.

We own a legacy of languages, poems, histories, and it is not one that will ever be exhausted. It is there, always.

We have a bequest of stories, tales from the old storytellers, some of whose names we know, but some not. The storytellers go back and back, to a clearing in the forest where a great fire burns, and the old shamans dance and sing, for our heritage of stories began in fire, magic, the spirit world. And that is where it is held, today.

Ask any modern storyteller and they will say there is always a moment when they are touched with fire, with what we like to call inspiration, and this goes back and back to the beginning of our race, to the great winds that shaped us and our world.

The storyteller is deep inside every one of us. The story-maker is always with us. Let us suppose our world is ravaged by war, by the horrors that we all of us easily imagine. Let us suppose floods wash through our cities, the seas rise. But the storyteller will be there, for it is our imaginations which shape us, keep us, create us – for good and for ill. It is our stories that will recreate us, when we are torn, hurt, even destroyed. It is the storyteller, the dream-maker, the myth-maker, that is our phoenix, that represents us at our best, and at our most creative.

That poor girl trudging through the dust, dreaming of an education for her children, do we think that we are better than she is – we, stuffed full of food, our cupboards full of clothes, stifling in our superfluities?

I think it is that girl, and the women who were talking about books and an education when they had not eaten for three days, that may yet define us.

Portrait photo of Doris Lessing by photographer Ulla Montan.

Literature 2008

**Jean-Marie Gustave Le Clézio**

"*author of new departures, poetic adventure and sensual ecstasy, explorer of a humanity beyond and below the reigning civilization*"

# THE NOBEL PRIZE IN LITERATURE

Speech by Professor Horace Engdahl of the Swedish Academy.
Translation of the Swedish text.

Your Majesties, Your Royal Highnesses, Ladies and Gentlemen,

Of what use are characters to a literary work? Roland Barthes maintained that the most antiquated of all literary conventions was the proper name – the Peter, Paul, and Anna who never existed but whom we are expected to take seriously and feel concerned about when we read novels. His view was in accordance with *le nouveau roman,* the new French novel, which at the time, forty years ago, was doing away with psychologically shaped characters, turning them into angles of vision, camera lenses.

In such a climate, Jean-Marie Le Clézio set out on his literary path. He writes in his second book, *La fièvre* (1965; *Fever*, 1966): "Poems, short stories and novels are antiquities that no longer fool anyone or just about. [...] All that is left is the writing, writing that gropes its way along with words that searches and describes, meticulously and in depth that clings on to and ruthlessly works over reality." The young Le Clézio was not alone in wanting to shake off the genres. But while his colleagues stressed doubt in the apprehensibility of reality, he chose to believe in the alliance of language with matter and the body.

His first novel, *Le procès-verbal (The Interrogation),* which made him a celebrity at the age of twenty-three, mixes confessions, parodies, diary fragments, found texts, newspaper items, word play, and dialogues from a mental hospital. In its feverish prose speaks a generation that has lost its faith in hierarchies. Everything that language captures seems equally valuable and equally instable. Le Clézio's early books are a verbal "big bang" with figures that appear and disappear, sudden bursts of light, vast silences, glowing matter, a universe in the making that continually dissolves its forms.

He could have stayed with prose poetry and crisis writing, heir of Lautréamont and Michaux and Stig Dagerman, if it had not been for his travels. A several year long stay in Central America brought him into contact with Indian culture, and this changed the conditions of his literary production. He discovered the denied knowledge that did not suit modernity and that progress had put in the shadows. He discovered that he was actually an Indian, but a poor one. In time, he would find a connection between this experience and his own family's history, his ancestors' migration to Mauritius, the struggle and the freedom at the ocean's edge. That cleared the way for masterpieces such as *Révolutions* and *L'Africain.*

This year's Laureate in Literature belongs to the tradition of the critique of civilisation, which on French ground can be traced back to Chateaubriand,

Bernardin de Saint-Pierre, Diderot, and yes, Montaigne. In the nineteen hundreds, it was represented with furious enthusiasm by Artaud, who Le Clézio follows in his relations with the old Mexican gods.

His books give a place of honour to eccentrics who have preserved the ties with their origin: gypsies, fishermen, ox drivers, nomads. He prefers groups in constant motion, those who live in our societies without belonging to them, and saves them from banality. Few authors have so convincingly described how reluctantly languages and cultures die. This is one of our time's unexpected experiences, which inspires hope and anguish in equal measure. The imprint of history does not fade. We do not become more like one another. The universally human is, for Le Clézio, the opposite of the international service type without a past encouraged in the Western capitals.

In the novel *Désert* (1980), which marked a new turn in his writing, the outsider position is represented by a Bedouin girl, who has left North Africa to look for work in France. She is an image of humanity before the Fall that came with the use of money. Unlearned, she reads the language of things with unerring certainty. An inborn remote gaze that defies time and place puts her in contact with her people's great past. Europe is seen in this novel through the eyes of the unwanted immigrants and appears as a realm of death.

The open form of this book has become typical for its author, a form that juxtaposes separate places, times, and discourses without mediation. In his hands, the novel merges with the travel story, the analytical essay, the prose of recollection, and witness literature. This alloy is strong enough to carry a consciousness that is open to global reality and does not merely pretend to be so in order to dominate it. Le Clézio gives us a French that has stepped down from the pedestal of purism and that is permeated by the consciousness of other languages.

And the proper names, the characters? In a very personal essay on cinema published just this year, Le Clézio describes how Jean Vigo expanded the language of film by shifting the focus from individuals to that which they see and experience. In the same way, fictive figures seem to find mercy in Le Clézio's writing when they appear, not so that we can immerse ourselves in their petty plots, but rather so that we can see with their eyes.

Le Clézio's imagination sustains itself in the unexplored regions where fear and ecstasy arise, inseparable from one another. It may seem surprising to call him a hopeful author, given the significant strain of colonial devastation, bourgeois oppressiveness, and social injustice in his themes. Still, he deserves such a designation. The earth's lustre, the sun, the sea, and the vast expanses, the irrepressible feeling of freedom that comes with a new departure – these are the forces that outweigh the sorrow about the path that our civilisation has taken.

Most honoured Laureate, dear Jean-Marie Le Clézio,

Your work is a story of migration; you are yourself a nomad of the world. You have in writing found a gateway to adventure, not as escapism, but as a hunger for the unknown. You have, after a long era in which the highest forms of expression seemed reserved for dystopian experience, restored to literature its power to celebrate the world. I would like to express the warm congratulations of the Swedish Academy as I now ask you to receive the Nobel Prize for Literature from the hands of His Majesty the King.

# JEAN-MARIE GUSTAVE LE CLÉZIO

J. M. G. Le Clézio was born in 1940 in Nice, France. He is a descendent of a Breton family that emigrated in the 18th century to Mauritius. He completed his undergraduate studies at the Institut d'Études Littéraires in Nice and is a Doctor of Philosophy.

Despite his extensive travels, since the age of seven or eight J.M.G. Le Clézio has never stopped writing: poems, sagas, tales, short stories, of which nothing was published until *Le Procès-verbal* (*The Interrogation*), his first novel, appeared in print in September 1963, for which he received Le Prix Renaudot. In 1980 he received Le Grand Prix Paul-Morand from the French Academy for his novel *Désert.*

In 2008 he was awarded the Nobel Prize in Literature.

# IN THE FOREST OF PARADOXES

Nobel Lecture, December 7, 2008

by

JEAN-MARIE GUSTAVE Le CLÉZIO

26, rue Jacob, F-75006 Paris, France.

Why do we write? I imagine that each of us has his or her own response to this simple question. One has predispositions, a milieu, circumstances. Shortcomings, too. If we are writing, it means that we are not acting. That we find ourselves in difficulty when we are faced with reality, and so we have chosen another way to react, another way to communicate, a certain distance, a time for reflection.

If I examine the circumstances which inspired me to write – and this is not mere self-indulgence, but a desire for accuracy – I see clearly that the starting point of it all for me was war. Not war in the sense of a specific time of major upheaval, where historical events are experienced, such as the French campaign on the battlefield at Valmy, as recounted by Goethe on the German side and my ancestor François on the side of the *armée révolutionnaire*. That must have been a moment full of exaltation and pathos. No, for me war is what civilians experience, very young children first and foremost. Not once has war ever seemed to me to be an historical moment. We were hungry, we were frightened, we were cold, and that is all. I remember seeing the troops of Field Marshal Rommel pass by under my window as they headed towards the Alps, seeking a passage to the north of Italy and Austria. I do not have a particularly vivid memory of that event. I do recall, however, that during the years which followed the war we were deprived of everything, in particular books and writing materials. For want of paper and ink, I made my first drawings and wrote my first texts on the back of the ration books, using a carpenter's blue and red pencil. This left me with a certain preference for rough paper and ordinary pencils. For want of any children's books, I read my grandmother's dictionaries. They were like a marvellous gateway, through which I embarked on a discovery of the world, to wander and daydream as I looked at the illustrated plates, and the maps and the lists of unfamiliar words. The first book I wrote, at the age of six or seven, was entitled, moreover, *Le Globe à mariner*. Immediately afterwards came a biography of an imaginary king named Daniel III – could he have been Swedish? – and a tale told by a seagull. It was a time of reclusion. Children were scarcely allowed outdoors to play, because in the fields and gardens near my grandmother's there were land mines. I recall that one day as I was out walking by the sea I came across an enclosure surrounded by barbed wire: on the fence was a sign in French and in German that threatened intruders with a forbidding message, and a skull to make things perfectly clear.

It is easy, in such a context, to understand the urge to escape – hence, to dream, and put those dreams in writing. My maternal grandmother, moreover, was an extraordinary storyteller, and she set aside the long afternoons for the telling of stories. They were always very imaginative, and were set in a forest – perhaps it was in Africa, or in Mauritius, the forest of Macchabée – where the main character was a monkey who had a great talent for mischief, and who always wriggled his way out of the most perilous situations. Later, I would travel to Africa and spend time there, and discover the real forest, one where there were almost no animals. But a District Officer in the village of Obudu, near the border with Cameroon, showed me how to listen for the drumming of the gorillas on a nearby hill, pounding their chests. And from that journey, and the time I spent there (in Nigeria, where my father was a bush doctor), it was not subject matter for future novels that I brought back, but a sort of second personality, a daydreamer who was fascinated with reality at the same time, and this personality has stayed with me all my life – and has constituted a contradictory dimension, a strangeness in myself that at times has been a source of suffering. Given the slowness of life, it has taken me the better part of my existence to understand the significance of this contradiction.

Books entered my life at a later period. When my father's inheritance was divided, at the time of his expulsion from the family home in Moka, in Mauritius, he managed to put together several libraries consisting of the books that remained. It was then that I understood a truth not immediately apparent to children, that books are a treasure more precious than any real property or bank account. It was in those volumes – most of them ancient, bound tomes – that I discovered the great works of world literature: *Don Quijote*, illustrated by Tony Johannot; *La vida de Lazarillo de Tormes;* the *Ingoldsby Legends; Gulliver's Travels;* Victor Hugo's great, inspired novels *Quatre-vingt-treize, Les Travailleurs de la Mer,* and *L'Homme qui rit.* Balzac's *Les Contes drolatiques,* as well. But the books which had the greatest impact on me were the anthologies of travellers' tales, most of them devoted to India, Africa and the Mascarene islands, or the great histories of exploration by Dumont d'Urville or the Abbé Rochon, as well as Bougainville, Cook, and of course *The Travels of Marco Polo.* In the mediocre life of a little provincial town dozing in the sun, after those years of freedom in Africa, those books gave me a taste for adventure, gave me a sense of the vastness of the real world, a means to explore it through instinct and the senses rather than through knowledge. In a way, too, those books gave me, from very early on, an awareness of the contradictory nature of a child's existence: a child will cling to a sanctuary, a place to forget violence and competitiveness, and also take pleasure in looking through the windowpane to watch the outside world go by.

Shortly before I received the – to me, astonishing – news that the Swedish Academy was awarding me this distinction, I was re-reading a little book by Stig Dagerman that I am particularly fond of: a collection of political essays entitled *Essäer och texter.* It was no mere chance that I was re-reading this bitter, abrasive book. I was preparing a trip to Sweden to receive the prize which the Association of the Friends of Stig Dagerman had awarded to me the previous summer, to visit the places where the writer had lived as a child. I have always been particularly receptive to Dagerman's writing, to the way in which he combines a child-like tenderness with naïveté and sarcasm. And to his idealism. To the clear-sightedness with which he judges his troubled, post-war era – that of his mature years, and of my childhood. One sentence in particular caught my attention, and seemed to be addressed to me at that very moment, for I had just published a novel entitled *Ritournelle de la faim.* That sentence, or that passage rather, is as follows: *"How is it possible on the one hand, for example, to behave as if nothing on earth were more important than literature, and on the other fail to see that wherever one looks, people are struggling against hunger and will necessarily consider that the most important thing is what they earn at the end of the month? Because this is where he (the writer) is confronted with a new paradox: while all he wanted was to write for those who are hungry, he now discovers that it is only those who have plenty to eat who have the leisure to take notice of his existence." (The Writer and Consciousness)*

This "forest of paradoxes", as Stig Dagerman calls it, is precisely the realm of writing, the place from which the artist must not attempt to escape: on the contrary, he or she must "camp out" there in order to examine every detail, explore every path, name every tree. It is not always a pleasant stay. He thought he had found shelter, she was confiding in her page as if it were a close, indulgent friend; but now these writers are confronted with reality, not merely as observers, but as actors. They must choose sides, establish their distance. Cicero, Rabelais, Condorcet, Rousseau, Madame de Staël or, far more recently, Solzhenitsyn or Hwang Sok-yong, Abdelatif Laâbi or Milan Kundera: all were obliged to follow the path of exile. For someone like myself who has always – except during that brief war-time period – enjoyed freedom of movement, the idea that one might be forbidden to live in the place one has chosen is as inadmissible as being deprived of one's freedom.

But the privilege of freedom of movement results in the paradox. Look, for a moment, at the tree with its prickly thorns that is at the very heart of the forest where the writer lives: this man, this woman, busily writing, inventing their dreams – do they not belong to a very fortunate and exclusive *happy few*? Let us pause and imagine an extreme, terrifying situation – like the one in which the vast majority of people on our planet find themselves. A situation which, long ago, at the time of Aristotle, or Tolstoy, was shared by those who had no status – serfs, servants, villeins in Europe in the Middle Ages, or those peoples who during the Enlightenment were plundered from the coast of Africa, sold in Gorée, or El Mina, or Zanzibar. And even today, as I am speaking to you, there are all those who do not have freedom of speech, who are on the other side of language. I am overcome by Dagerman's pessimistic thoughts, rather than by Gramsci's militancy, or Sartre's disillusioned wager. The idea that literature is the luxury of a dominant class, feeding on ideas and images that remain foreign to the vast majority: that is the source of the malaise that each of us is feeling – as I address those who read, who write. Of course one would like to spread the word to all those who have been excluded, to invite them magnanimously to the banquet of culture. Why is this so difficult? Peoples without writing, as the anthropologists like to call them, have succeeded in inventing a form of total communication, through song and myth. Why has this become impossible for our industrialised societies, in the present day? Must we reinvent culture? Must we return to an immediate, direct form of communication? It is tempting to believe that the cinema fulfils just such a role in our time, or popular music with its rhythms and rhymes, its echoes of the dance. Or jazz and, in other climes, calypso, maloya, sega.

The paradox is not a recent one. François Rabelais, the greatest writer in the French language, waged war long ago against the pedantry of the scholars at the Sorbonne by taunting them to their face with words plucked from the common tongue. Was he speaking for those who were hungry? Excess, intoxication, feasting. He put into words the extraordinary appetite of those who dined off the emaciation of peasants and workers, just long enough for a masquerade, a world turned upside down. The paradox of revolution, like the epic cavalcade of the sad-faced knight, lives within the writer's consciousness. If there is one virtue which the writer's pen must always have, it is that it must never be used to praise the powerful, even with the faintest of scribblings. And yet just because an artist observes this virtuous behaviour does not mean that he may feel purged of all suspicion. His rebellion, denial and imprecations definitely remain to one side of the barrier, the side of the language of power. A few words, a few phrases may have escaped. But the rest? A long palimpsest, an elegant and distant time of procrastination. And there is humour, sometimes, which is not the politeness of despair, but the despairing of those who know too well their imperfections; humour is the shore where the tumultuous current of injustice has abandoned them.

Why write, then? For some time now, writers have no longer been so presumptuous as to believe that they can change the world, that they will, through their stories and novels, give birth to a better example for how life should be. Simply, they would like to bear witness. Now, see that other tree in the forest of paradoxes the writer would like to bear witness, when in fact, most of the time, he is nothing more than a simple voyeur.

And yet there are artists who do become witnesses: Dante in the *La Divina Commedia*, Shakespeare in *The Tempest* – and Aimé Césaire in his magnificent adaptation of that play, entitled *Une Tempête*, in which Caliban, sitting astride a barrel of gunpowder, threatens to blow himself up and take his despised masters with him. There are also those witnesses who are unimpeachable, such as Euclides da Cunha in *Os Sertões*, or Primo Levi. We see the absurdity of the world in *Der Prozess* (or in the films of Charlie Chaplin); its imperfection in Colette's *La Naissance du jour*, its phantasmagoria in the Irish ballad Joyce created in *Finnegans Wake*. Its beauty shines, brilliantly, irresistibly, in Peter Matthiessen's *The Snow Leopard* or in Aldo Leopold's *A Sand County Almanac*. Its wickedness in William Faulkner's *Sanctuary*, or in Lao She's *First Snow*. Its childhood fragility in Dagerman's *Ormen* (*The Snake*).

The best writer as witness is the one who is a witness in spite of himself, unwillingly. The paradox is that he does not bear witness to something he has seen, or even to what he has invented. Bitterness, even despair may arise because he cannot be present at the indictment. Tolstoy may show us the suffering that Napoleon's army inflicted upon Russia, and yet nothing is changed in the course of history. Claire de Duras wrote *Ourika,* and Harriet Beecher Stowe *Uncle Tom's Cabin,* but it was the enslaved peoples themselves who changed their own destiny, who rebelled and fought against injustice by creating the Maroon resistance in Brazil, in French Guiana, and in the West Indies, and the first black republic in Haiti.

To act: that is what the writer would like to be able to do, above all. To act, rather than to bear witness. To write, imagine, and dream in such a way that his words and inventions and dreams will have an impact upon reality, will change people's minds and hearts, will prepare the way for a better world. And yet, at that very moment, a voice is whispering to him that it will not be possible, that words are words that are taken away on the winds of society, and dreams are mere illusions. What right has he to wish he were better? Is it really up to the writer to try to find solutions? Is he not in the position of the gamekeeper in the play *Knock ou Le Triomphe de la médecine,* who would like to prevent an earthquake? How can the writer act, when all he knows is how to remember?

Solitude will be his lot in life. It always has been. As a child, he was a fragile, anxious, excessively receptive boy, or the girl described by Colette, who cannot help but watch as her parents tear each other apart, her big black eyes enlarged with a sort of painful attentiveness. Solitude is affectionate to writers, and it is in the company of solitude that they find the essence of happiness. It is a contradictory happiness, a mixture of pain and delight, an illusory triumph, a muted, omnipresent torment, not unlike a haunting little tune. The writer, better than anyone, knows how to cultivate the vital, poisonous plant, the one that grows only in the soil of his own powerlessness. The writer wanted to speak for everyone, and for every era: there he is, there she is, each alone in a room, facing the too-white mirror of the blank page, beneath the lampshade distilling its secret light. Or sitting at the too-bright screen of the computer, listening to the sound of one's fingers clicking over the keys. This, then, is the writer's forest. And each writer knows every path in that forest all too well. If, now and again, something escapes, like a bird flushed by a dog at dawn, then the writer looks on, amazed – this happened merely by chance, in spite of oneself.

It is not my wish, however, to revel in negativity. Literature – and this is what I have been driving at – is not some archaic relic that ought, logically, to be replaced by the audiovisual arts, the cinema in particular. Literature is a complex, difficult path, but I hold it to be even more vital today than in the time of Byron or Victor Hugo.

There are two reasons why literature is necessary: First of all, because literature is made up of language. The primary sense of the word: letters, that which is written. In French, the word *roman* refers to those texts in prose which for the first time after the Middle Ages used the new language spoken by the people, a Romance language. And the word for short story, *nouvelle*, also derives from this notion of novelty. At roughly the same time, in France, the word *rimeur* (from *rime*, or rhyme) fell out of use for designating poetry and poets – the new words come from the Greek verb *poiein*, to create. The writer, the poet, the novelist are all creators. This does not mean that they invent language, it means that they use language to create beauty, ideas, images. This is why we cannot do without them. Language is the most extraordinary invention in the history of humanity, the one which came before everything and which makes it possible to share everything. Without language there would be no science, no technology, no law, no art, no love. But without another person with whom to interact, the invention becomes virtual. It may atrophy, diminish, disappear. Writers, to a certain degree, are the guardians of language. When they write their novels, their poetry, their plays, they keep language alive. They are not merely using words – on the contrary, they are at the service of language. They celebrate it, hone it, transform it, because language lives through them and because of them, and it accompanies all the social and economic transformations of their era.

When, in the last century, racist theories were expressed, there was talk of fundamental differences between cultures. In a sort of absurd hierarchy, a correlation was drawn between the economic success of the colonial powers and their purported cultural superiority. Such theories, like a feverish, unhealthy urge, tend to resurface here and there, now and again, to justify neocolonialism or imperialism. There are, we are told, certain nations that lag behind, which have not acquired their rights and privileges where language is concerned, because they are economically backward or technologically outdated. But have those who proclaim their cultural superiority realised that all peoples, the world over, whatever their degree of development, use language? And that each of these languages has, identically, a set of logical, complex, structured, analytical features that enable it to express the world, that enable it to speak of science or invent myths?

Now that I have defended the existence of that ambiguous and somewhat passé creature we call a writer, I would like to turn to the second reason for the necessity of literature, for this has more to do with the fine profession of publishing.

There is a great deal of talk about globalisation these days. People forget that in fact the phenomenon began in Europe during the Renaissance, with the beginnings of the colonial era. Globalisation is not a bad thing in and of itself. Communication has accelerated progress in medicine and in science. Perhaps the generalisation of information will help to forestall conflicts. Who knows, if the Internet had existed at the time, perhaps Hitler's criminal plot would not have succeeded – ridicule might have prevented it from ever seeing the light of day.

We live in the era of the Internet and virtual communication. This is a good thing, but what would these astonishing inventions be worth, were it not for the teachings of written language and books? To provide nearly everyone on the planet with a liquid crystal display is utopian. Are we not, therefore, in the process of creating a new elite, of drawing a new line to divide the world between those who have access to communication and knowledge, and those who are left out? Great nations, great civilisations have vanished because they failed to realise that this could happen. To be sure, there are great cultures, considered to be in a minority, which have been able to resist until this day, thanks to the oral transmission of knowledge and myths. It is indispensable, and beneficial, to acknowledge the contribution of these cultures. But whether we like it or not, even if we have not yet attained the age of reality, we are no longer living in the age of myths. It is not possible to provide a foundation for equality and the respect of others unless each child receives the benefits of writing.

And now, in this era following decolonisation, literature has become a way for the men and women in our time to express their identity, to claim their right to speak, and to be heard in all their diversity. Without their voices, their call, we would live in a world of silence.

Culture on a global scale concerns us all. But it is above all the responsibility of readers – of publishers, in other words. True, it is unjust that an Indian from the far north of Canada, if he wishes to be heard, must write in the language of the conquerors – in French, or in English. True, it is an illusion to expect that the Creole language of Mauritius or the West Indies might be heard as easily around the world as the five or six languages that reign today as absolute monarchs over the media. But if, through translation, their voices can be heard, then something new is happening, a cause for optimism. Culture, as I have said, belongs to us all, to all humankind. But in order for this to be true, everyone must be given equal access to culture. The book, however old-fashioned it may be, is the ideal tool. It is practical, easy to handle, economical. It does not require any particular technological prowess, and keeps well in any climate. Its only flaw – and this is where I would like to address publishers in particular – is that in a great number of countries it is still very difficult to gain access to books. In Mauritius the price of a novel or a collection of poetry is equivalent to a sizeable portion of the family budget. In Africa, South East Asia, Mexico, or the South Sea Islands, books remain an inaccessible luxury. And yet remedies to this situation do exist. Joint publication with the developing countries, the establishment of funds for lending libraries and bookmobiles, and, overall, greater attention to requests from and works in so-called minority languages – which are often clearly in the majority – would enable literature to continue to be this wonderful tool for self-knowledge, for the discovery of others and for listening to the concert of humankind, in all the rich variety of its themes and modulations.

I think I would like to say a few more words about the forest. It is no doubt for this reason that Stig Dagerman's little sentence is still echoing in my memory, and for this reason that I want to read it and re-read it, to fill myself with it. There is a note of despair in his words, and something triumphant at the same time, because it is in bitterness that we can find the grain of truth that each of us seeks. As a child, I dreamt of that forest. It frightened me and fascinated me at the same time – I suppose that Tom Thumb and Hansel must have felt that way, when they were deep in the forest, surrounded by all its dangers and its wonders. The forest is a world without landmarks. You can get lost in the thickness of trees and the impenetrable darkness. The same could be said of the desert, or the open ocean, where every dune, every hill gives way to yet another identical hill, every wave to yet another perfectly identical wave. I remember the first time I experienced just what literature could be – in Jack London's *The Call of the Wild*, to be exact, where one of the characters, lost in the snow, felt the cold gaining on him just as the circle of wolves was closing round him. He looked at his hand, which was already numb, and tried to move each finger one after the other. There was something magical in this discovery for me, as a child. It was called self-awareness.

To the forest I owe one of the greatest literary emotions of my adult life. This was about thirty years ago, in a region of Central America known as El Tapón del Darién, the Darién Gap, because that is where, in those days (and I believe the situation has not changed in the meantime), there was an interruption in the Pan-American Highway that was meant to join the two Americas from Alaska to the tip of Tierra del Fuego. In this region of the isthmus of Panama the rainforest is extremely dense, and the only means of travelling there is to go upriver by pirogue. In the forest there lives an indigenous population, divided into two groups, the Emberá and the Wounaans, both belonging to the Ge-Pano-Carib linguistic family. I had landed there by chance, and was so fascinated by this people that I stayed there several times for fairly lengthy periods, over roughly three years. During the entire time I did nothing other than wander aimlessly from one house to the next – for at the time the population refused to live in villages – and learn to live according to a rhythm that was completely different from anything I had known up to that point. Like all true forests, this forest was particularly hostile. I had to draw up a list of all the potential dangers, and of all the corresponding means of survival. I have to say that on the whole the Emberá were very patient with me. They were amused by my awkwardness, and I think that to a certain degree, I was able to repay them in entertainment what they shared with me in wisdom. I did not write a great deal. The rain forest is not really an ideal setting. Your paper gets soaked with the humidity, the heat dries out all your ball point pens. Nothing that has to work off electricity lasts for very long. I had arrived there with the conviction that writing was a privilege, and that I would always be able to resort to it in order to resolve all my existential problems. A protection, in a way; a sort of virtual window that I could roll up as I needed to shelter from the storm.

Once I had assimilated the system of primitive communism practised by the Amerindians, as well as their profound disgust for authority and their tendency towards natural anarchy, I came to see that art, as a form of individual expression, did not have any role to play in the forest. Besides, these people had nothing that resembled what we call art in our consumer society. Instead of hanging paintings on a wall, the men and women painted their bodies, and in general were loath to create anything lasting. And then I gained access to their myths. When we talk of myths, in our world of written books, it seems as if we are referring to something that is very far away, either in time, or in space. I too believed in that distance. And now suddenly the myths were there for me to hear, regularly, almost every night. Near the wood fire that people built in their houses on a hearth of three stones, amidst the dance of mosquitoes and moths, the voice of the storytellers – men and women alike – would set in motion stories, legends, tales, as if they were speaking of a daily reality. The storyteller sang in a shrill voice, striking his breast; his face would mime the expressions and passions and fears of the characters. It might have been something from a novel, not a myth. But one night, a young woman came. Her name was Elvira. She was known throughout the entire forest of the Emberá for her storytelling skills. She was an adventuress, and lived without a man, without children – people said that she was a bit of a drunkard, a bit of a whore, but I don't believe it for a minute – and she would go from house to house to sing, in exchange for a meal or a bottle of alcohol or sometimes a few coins. Although I had no access to her tales other than through translation – the Emberá language has a literary variant that is far more complex than the everyday form – I quickly realised that she was a great artist, in the best sense of the term. The timbre of her voice, the rhythm of her hands tapping against her chest, against her heavy necklaces of silver coins, and above all the air of possession which illuminated her face and her gaze, a sort of measured, rhythmic trance, exerted a power over all those who were present. To the simple framework of her myths – the invention of tobacco, the first primeval twins, stories about gods and humans from the dawn of time – she added her own story, her life of wandering, her loves, the betrayals and suffering, the intense joy of carnal love, the sting of jealousy, her fear of growing old, of dying. She was poetry in action, ancient theatre, and the most contemporary of novels all at the same time. She was all those things with fire, with violence; she invented, in the blackness of the forest, amidst the surrounding chorus of insects and toads and the whirlwind of bats, a sensation which cannot be called anything other than beauty. As if in her song she carried the true power of nature, and this was surely the greatest paradox: that this isolated place, this forest, as far away as could be imagined from the sophistication of literature, was the place where art had found its strongest, most authentic expression.

Then I left that region, and I never saw Elvira again, or any of the storytellers of the forest of Darién. But I was left with far more than nostalgia – with the certainty that literature could exist, even when it was worn away by convention and compromise, even if writers were incapable of changing the world. Something great and powerful, which surpassed them, which on occasion could enliven and transfigure them, and restore the sense of harmony with nature. Something new and very ancient at the same time, impalpable as the wind, ethereal as the clouds, infinite as the sea. It is this something which vibrates in the poetry of Jalal ad-Din Rumi, for example, or in the visionary architecture of Emanuel Swedenborg. The shiver one feels on reading the most beautiful texts of humankind, such as the speech that Chief Stealth gave in the mid-19th century to the President of the United States upon conceding his land: "We may be brothers after all…"

Something simple, and true, which exists in language alone. A charm, sometimes a ruse, a grating dance, or long spells of silence. The language of mockery, of interjections, of curses, and then, immediately afterwards, the language of paradise.

It is to her, to Elvira, that I address this tribute – and to her that I dedicate the Prize which the Swedish Academy is awarding me. To her and to all those writers with whom – or sometimes against whom – I have lived. To the Africans: Wole Soyinka, Chinua Achebe, Ahmadou Kourouma, Mongo Beti, to Alan Paton's *Cry the Beloved Country*, to Thomas Mofolo's *Chaka*. To the great Mauritian author Malcolm de Chazal, who wrote, among other things, *Judas*. To the Hindi-language Mauritian novelist Abhimanyu Unnuth, for *Lal passina* (*Sweating Blood*) to the Urdu novelist Qurratulain Hyder for her epic novel *Ag ka Darya* (*River of Fire*). To the defiant Danyèl Waro of La Réunion, for his maloya songs; to the Kanak poetess Déwé Gorodey, who defied the colonial powers all the way to prison; to the rebellious Abdourahman Waberi. To Juan Rulfo and *Pedro Paramo,* and his short stories *El llano en llamas,* and the simple and tragic photographs he took of rural Mexico. To John Reed for *Insurgent Mexico;* to Jean Meyer who was the spokesman for Aurelio Acevedo and the Cristeros insurgents of central Mexico. To Luis González, author of *Pueblo en vilo.* To John Nichols, who wrote about the bitter land of *The Milagro Beanfield War*; to Henry Roth, my neighbour on New York Street in Albuquerque, New Mexico, for *Call it Sleep.* To Jean-Paul Sartre, for the tears contained in his play *Morts sans sépulture.* To Wilfred Owen, the poet who died on the banks of the Marne in 1914. To J.D. Salinger, because he succeeded in putting us in the shoes of a young fifteen-year-old boy named Holden Caulfield. To the writers of the first nations in America – Sherman Alexie the Sioux, Scott Momaday the Navajo for *The Names.* To Rita Mestokosho, an Innu poet from Mingan, Quebec, who lends her voice to trees and animals. To José Maria Arguedas, Octavio Paz, Miguel Angel Asturias. To the poets of the oases of Oualata and Chinguetti. For their great imagination, to Alphonse Allais and Raymond Queneau. To Georges Perec for *Quel petit vélo à guidon chromé au fond de la cour?* To the erudit and poet Jean Grosjean. To the West Indian authors Edouard Glissant and Patrick Chamoiseau, to René Depestre from Haiti, to André Schwartz-Bart for *Le Dernier des justes.* To the Mexican poet Homero Aridjis who allows us to imagine the life of a leatherback turtle, and who evokes the rivers flowing orange with Monarch butterflies along the streets of his village, Contepec. To Vénus Koury Ghata who speaks of Lebanon as of a tragic, invincible lover. To Khalil Gibran. To Rimbaud. To Emile Nelligan. To Réjean Ducharme, for life.

To the unknown child I met one day, on the banks of the river Tuira, in the forest of Darién. At night, sitting on the floor in a shop, lit by the flame of a kerosene lamp, he is reading a book and writing, hunched forward, not paying the slightest attention to anything around him, oblivious of the discomfort or noise or promiscuity of the harsh, violent life there just next to him. That child sitting cross-legged on the floor of that shop, in the heart of the forest, reading all alone in the lamplight, is not there by chance. He resembles like a brother that other child I spoke about at the beginning of these pages, who was trying to write with a carpenter's pencil on the back of ration books, in the dark years immediately after the war. The child reminds us of the two great urgent tasks of human history, tasks we are far, alas, from having fulfilled. The eradication of hunger, and the elimination of illiteracy.

For all his pessimism, Stig Dagerman's phrase about the fundamental paradox of the writer, unsatisfied because he cannot communicate with those who are hungry – whether for nourishment or for knowledge – touches on the greatest truth. Literacy and the struggle against hunger are connected, closely interdependent. One cannot succeed without the other. Both of them require, indeed urge, us to act. So that in this third millennium, which has only just begun, no child on our shared planet, regardless of gender or language or religion, shall be abandoned to hunger or ignorance, or turned away from the feast. This child carries within him the future of our human race. In the words of the Greek philosopher Heraclitus, a very long time ago, the kingdom belongs to a child.

Translated from French by Alison Anderson.

Portrait photo of Jean-Marie Gustave Le Clézio by photographer Ulla Montan.

Literature 2009

**Herta Müller**

*"who, with the concentration of poetry and the frankness of prose, depicts the landscape of the dispossessed"*

# THE NOBEL PRIZE IN LITERATURE

Speech by Professor Anders Olsson of the Swedish Academy.
Translation of the Swedish text

*Your Majesties, Your Royal Highnesses, Ladies and Gentlemen,*

Some literature reveals its deep qualities slowly, step by step. Other literature captures the reader immediately by its resolute address. Herta Müller's work belongs in the latter category. Her prose has a linguistic energy that we bond with from the first sentence. Something concerning life or death is at stake. We sense this quickly through the temperature, the hurried breathing, the sharp detail, and everything implied but left unsaid.

This energy springs from a refusal to accept what is. Herta Müller chooses opposition as method, making common cause with the Austrian author, Thomas Bernhard. But, even more strongly than Bernhard's, her work is anchored in her own experience. She has said that her subjects have chosen her, not the other way around. Almost everything she writes is about life under Ceaușescu's Romanian dictatorship, its fear and betrayal and constant surveillance.

But Herta Müller has also portrayed a kind of dictatorship within a dictatorship: the small, German-speaking rural society in western Romania where she grew up. We enter it in her first book *Niederungen*, 1983 (*Nadirs*, 1999) a suite as cruel as luminous images to a child's gaping senses. Out steps an alien ego, its alienation also self-induced through a transformative, critical gaze. In the visionary short prose of *Barfüssiger Februar* from 1987, a dream image such as the black axis deep down at the bottom of the well captures, with hallucinatory strength, the way a village existence orbits life and death.

Quickly, the exposition of alienation widens into the Romanian dictatorship in general. This happens especially after Herta Müller is forced into exile in Germany in 1987 after years of censorship, interrogation and harassment. It can be said that in her case, exile serves to sharpen the confrontation with dictatorship. This occurs in novels such as: *Der Fuchs war damals schon der Jäger* from 1992, with its shining series of images of everyday terror; *Herztier*, 1994 (*The Land of Green Plums*, 1996) a masterful account of the flight of a group of youths from the terror regime; or *Heute wär ich mir lieber nicht begegnet*, 1997 (*The Appointment*, 2001) a fractured, chilling thriller in the shadow of imminent interrogation.

Herta Müller's experience of oppression leaves her no peace. But central to her art are figures of opposition. In a famous essay, Claudio Guillén coined the word 'counter-exile' for writers not defeated by exile through nostalgia. For Herta Müller, doubly rootless, return is an impossibility. The nostalgia is unconscious, flickering through only in the shape of a lone apricot tree on an embankment, so foreign in Berlin's northern latitudes. As so often, objects show Herta Müller a direction. They play a major part in her prose, because their shadow-side points to the labyrinths of fear.

Herta Müller has said that her German-speaking upbringing in Romania has been a great inspiration to her writing. For a writer it can be invaluable to have two different languages, and from this situation she early learned to compare, to turn and twist words to extract new meanings.

You find, in Herta Müller's prose, no epic line, no plot with beginning and end. If the world is ambiguous and opaque, literature must cease to provide a deceptive overview of it. She has said that only fictional surprise allows us to approach reality. She scissors out bits of experience to subsequently amalgamate them, and she has also used collage as a method to write poetry. In her essay collection, *Der König verneigt sich und tötet* from 2003, an indispensable guideline to her authorship, she explains that she finds no conclusive difference between poetry and prose. Her individuality as a narrator resides in just that ability to marry poetry's density with the feel for detail in prose. She does this in crystal-clear syntax, where every clause demands our attention.

With infinite empathy and unsentimental eye, she prolongs her counter-exile in her great novel *Atemschaukel* from 2009, about the deportation of Romanian-Germans from the year 1945 and their forced labour in what was then the Soviet Union. Here, she is pursuing the project planned with her close friend, the poet Oskar Pastior, who died in 2006. When young, Pastior had been in a Soviet camp. Even here, in stronger dependency than earlier on documentary material, she succeeds in uniting the lucidity of prose with the shock impact of poetic imagery. In the vivid coinage of the title, *Atemschaukel*, translatable as "Breathswing", she is heir to the great Romanian-German exile poet Paul Celan, who could call one of his collections *Atemwende*, "Breathturn". In intensive, intermittent episodes from camp life, she gives a segment of unavoidable contemporary history renewed visibility.

Liebe Herta Müller,

Sie haben den großen Mut gehabt die provinzielle Unterdrückung und den politischen Terror kompromißlos Widerstand geleistet. Es ist für den künstlerischen Gehalt dieses Widerstands, daß Sie diesen Preis verdienen. Ihr Werk ist ein Kampf der fortgeht und fortgehen muß, eine Form des unwiderruflichen Gegen-Exils. Und obwohl Sie gesagt haben, daß Sie das Schreiben vom Schweigen und Verschweigen gelernt haben, haben Sie uns Wörter gegeben die uns unmittelbar und tief ergreifen – mit dem Schweigen, über dem Schweigen. Ich möchte die wärmsten Glückwünsche der Schwedischen Akademie aussprechen, wenn ich Sie jetzt auffordere, den Nobelpreis für Literatur aus der Hand Seiner Majestät des Königs entgegenzunehmen.

'Dear Herta Müller,

You have shown great courage in uncompromisingly repudiating provincial repression and political terror. It is for the artistic value in that opposition that you merit this prize. Your work is a labour that continues and must continue a form of irreversible counter-exile. And even though you have said that silence and suppression taught you to write, you have given us words that grip us deeply and directly – in silence and beyond silence. I would like to express the warmest congratulations of the Swedish Academy as I now request you to receive the Nobel Prize for Literature from the hands of His Majesty the King.'

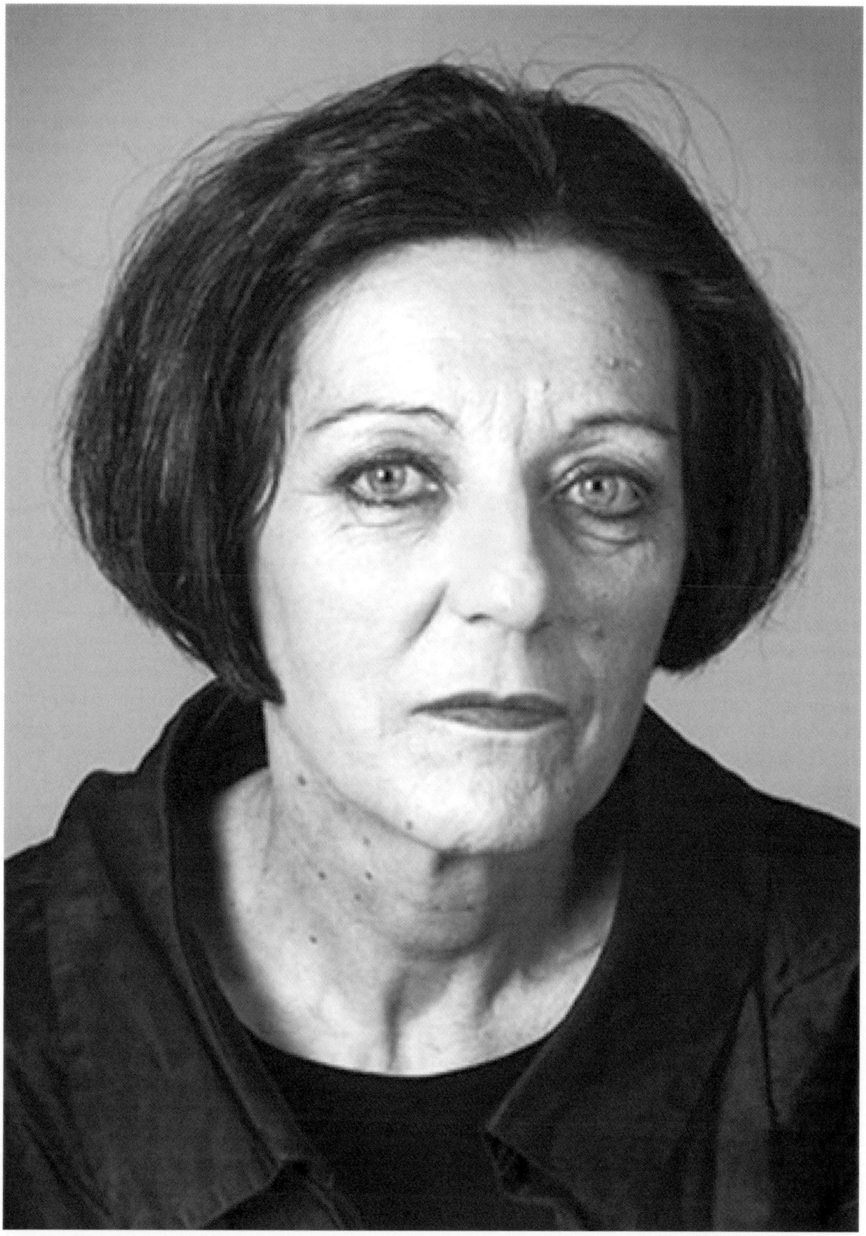

# HERTA MÜLLER

Herta Müller was born in 1953 in Nitzkydorf, a German-speaking village in the Banat, a region that had passed from the Austro-Hungarian Empire to Romania in the wake of the First World War. During the Second World War, Romania had allied with the National-Socialist German Reich, and like many of the Romanian-Germans, Herta Müller's father volunteered for Hitler's Waffen-SS. Shortly before the end of the war Romania changed positions, and in January 1945, while the fighting was still on, Stalin ordered all Romanian-Germans between the ages of 17 and 45 to be deported to the Soviet Union to perform five years of forced labor. Among them was Herta Müller's mother.

From 1973 to 1976, Herta Müller studied Romanian and German literature in Timişoara, where she befriended authors from the "Aktionsgruppe Banat," a group of writers opposed to the Ceauşescu dictatorship and the official literature of the ruling socialist party. For Herta Müller, her father's service as an SS soldier in the "Panzer Division Frundsberg" provided a frightening example of how individuals can be corrupted by ideology and opportunism - and inoculated her at a young age against similar structures within the communist ideology. Upon completing her studies, Herta Müller worked as a translator in a machine factory in Timişoara. In 1979 she was approached by the Romanian secret police (Securitate), but she refused to spy on her colleagues and foreign guests, and as a result she lost her job and could only find occasional employment.

Her first book *Niederungen* (English title: *Nadirs*) dates from this period, although it wasn't until 1982 that a censored version appeared in Romania. In 1984 she published a collection of short prose in Romania entitled *Drückender Tango*; that same year an uncensored but abridged edition of *Niederungen* came out in Germany, making her name as a writer overnight. Told from the perspective of a young girl, with all her fantasies and fears, the book depicts the confinement, corruption, intolerance, and oppression of a Swabian village in the Banat. In the German media, Herta Müller openly criticized the communist dictatorship: as a result she was prohibited from publishing and repeatedly summoned by the Securitate for interrogations, where she was confronted with absurd accusations, reviled as a prostitute, charged with black marketeering, and threatened with death. In 1987 she emigrated to Germany together with writer Richard Wagner, her husband at the time. Since then she has lived in Berlin.

Even there, however, she was persecuted and threatened by the Securitate, in the perfidious manner described in her 2009 book *Cristina und ihre Attrappe* which is based on materials in her secret police file the author was able to obtain. The dossier revealed that only her reputation in Germany protected her from a trial that had already been prepared, on the trumped-up charge of being a foreign agent.

In the first book she wrote in Germany, which appeared in 1989 as *Reisende auf einem Bein* (English title: *Traveling on One Leg*), she portrayed the difficulties of finding a foothold in strange surroundings. Other novels followed about daily life in a dictatorship, difficult friendships, and the long arm of the secret police reaching into the private sphere - such as her 1994 book *Herztier* (English title: *The Land of Green Plums*) or the 1997 *Heute wär ich mir lieber nicht begegnet* (English title: *The Appointment*). Further publications include essays on her own poetics (*Der König verneigt sich und tötet*, 2003) and several volumes of collages combining images and text, most recently *Die blassen Herren mit den Mokkatassen* (2005).

In 2009 she published the novel *Atemschaukel*, about the deportation of the Romanian-German minority to the Soviet Union. Originally she wanted to write this novel together with the poet Oskar Pastior, who himself had been deported for five years of forced labor in what is now Ukraine. It is his detailed recollections that provide the basis of the novel. While they were still in the preparatory phase, Oskar Pastior died, and Herta Müller was forced to write the book alone. *Atemschaukel* is not only a moving depiction of the unknown deportation of the Romanian-Germans; in the voice of the protagonist Leo Auberg, it is also Herta Müller's literary monument to Oskar Pastior.

# EVERY WORD KNOWS SOMETHING OF A VICIOUS CIRCLE

Nobel Lecture, December 7, 2009

by

HERTA MÜLLER

Berlin, Germany.

DO YOU HAVE A HANDKERCHIEF was the question my mother asked me every morning, standing by the gate to our house, before I went out onto the street. I didn't have a handkerchief. And because I didn't, I would go back inside and get one. I never had a handkerchief because I would always wait for her question. The handkerchief was proof that my mother was looking after me in the morning. For the rest of the day I was on my own. The question DO YOU HAVE A HANDKERCHIEF was an indirect display of affection. Anything more direct would have been embarrassing and not something the farmers practiced. Love disguised itself as a question. That was the only way it could be spoken: matter-of-factly, in the tone of a command, or the deft maneuvers used for work. The brusqueness of the voice even emphasized the tenderness. Every morning I went to the gate once without a handkerchief and a second time with a handkerchief. Only then would I go out onto the street, as if having the handkerchief meant having my mother there, too.

Twenty years later I had been on my own in the city a long time and was working as a translator in a manufacturing plant. I would get up at five a.m.; work began at six-thirty. Every morning the loudspeaker blared the national anthem into the factory yard; at lunch it was the workers' choruses. But the workers simply sat over their meals with empty tinplate eyes and hands smeared with oil. Their food was wrapped in newspaper. Before they ate their bit of fatback, they first scraped the newsprint off the rind. Two years went by in the same routine, each day like the next.

In the third year the routine came to an end. Three times in one week a visitor showed up at my office early in the morning: an enormous, thick-boned man with sparkling blue eyes – a colossus from the Securitate.

The first time he stood there, cursed me, and left.

The second time he took off his windbreaker, hung it on the key to the cabinet, and sat down. That morning I had brought some tulips from home and arranged them in a vase. The man looked at me and praised me for being such a keen judge of character. His voice was slippery. I felt uneasy.

I contested his praise and assured him that I understood tulips, but not people. Then he said maliciously that he knew me better than I knew tulips. After that he draped his windbreaker over his arm and left.

The third time he sat down but I stayed standing, because he had set his briefcase on my chair. I didn't dare move it to the floor. He called me stupid, said I was a shirker and a slut, as corrupted as a stray bitch. He shoved the tulips close to the edge of the desk, then put an empty sheet of paper and a pen in the middle of the desktop. He yelled at me: Write. Without sitting down, I wrote what he dictated – my name, date of birth and address. Next, that I would tell no one, no matter how close a friend or relative, that I… and then came the terrible word: *colaborez – I am collaborating.* At that point I stopped writing. I put down the pen and went to the window and looked out onto the dusty street, unpaved and full of potholes, and at all the hump-backed houses. On top of everything else this street was called Strada Gloriei – Glory Street. On Glory Street a cat was sitting in a bare mulberry tree. It was the factory cat with the torn ear. And above the cat the early morning sun was shining like a yellow drum. I said: *N-am caracterul – I don't have the character for this.* I said it to the street outside. The word CHARACTER made the Securitate man hysterical. He tore up the sheet of paper and threw the pieces on the floor. Then he probably realized he would have to show his boss that he had tried to recruit me, because he bent over, picked up the scraps and tossed them into his briefcase. After that he gave a deep sigh and, defeated, hurled the vase with the tulips against the wall. As it shattered it made a grinding sound, as though the air had teeth. With his briefcase under his arm he said quietly: *You'll be sorry, we'll drown you in the river.* I said as if to myself: *If I sign that, I won't be able to live with myself anymore, and I'll have to do it on my own. So it's better if you do it.* By then the office door was already open and he was gone. And outside on the Strada Gloriei the factory cat had jumped from the tree onto the roof of the building. One branch was bouncing like a trampoline.

The next day the tug of war began. They wanted me out of the factory. Every morning at 6:30 I had to report to the director. The head of the official labor union and the party secretary were also in his office. Just like my mother once asked: DO YOU HAVE A HANDKERCHIEF, the director now asked every morning: Have you found another job? Every morning I gave the same answer: *I'm not looking for one, I like it here in the factory, I'd like to stay here until I retire.*

One morning I came to work and found my thick dictionaries lying on the floor of the hall outside my office. I opened the door; an engineer was sitting at my desk. He said: *People are supposed to knock before they enter a room. This is my place, you have no business here.* I couldn't go home; any unexcused absence would have given them a pretext to fire me. I no longer had an office, so now I really had to make sure I came to work; under no circumstances could I fail to be there.

My friend, whom I told everything as we walked home down the pitiful Strada Gloriei, cleared a corner of her desk for me, at first. But one morning she stood outside her office and said: *I can't let you in. Everyone is saying you're an informer.* The harassment was passed down; the rumor was set into circulation among my colleagues. That was the worst. You can defend yourself against an attack, but there's nothing you can do against libel. Every day I prepared myself for anything, including death. But I couldn't cope with this perfidy. No preparation made it bearable. Libel stuffs you with filth; you suffocate because you can't defend yourself. In the eyes of my colleagues I was exactly what I had refused to become. If I had spied on them they would have trusted me without the slightest hesitation. In essence they were punishing me because I had spared them.

Since now I really had to make sure I came to work, but no longer had an office, and since my friend could no longer let me into hers, I stood in the stairwell, unable to decide what to do. I climbed up and down the stairs a few times and suddenly I was again my mother's child, because I HAD A HANDKERCHIEF. I placed it on one of the stairs between the second and third floors, carefully smoothed it out and sat down. I rested my thick dictionaries on my knee and translated the descriptions of hydraulic machines. I was a staircase wit and my office was a handkerchief. My friend joined me on the stairs at lunchtime. We ate together as we had in her office, and before that in mine. From the loudspeaker in the yard the workers' choruses sang about the happiness of the people, as always. My friend ate her lunch and cried over me. I didn't cry. I had to stay tough. For a long time. A few never-ending weeks, until I was dismissed.

During the time that I was a staircase wit, I looked up the word STAIR in the dictionary: the first step is the STARTING STEP or CURTAIL STEP that can also be a BULLNOSE. HAND is the direction a stair takes at the first riser. The edge of a tread that projects past the face of the riser is called the NOSING. I already knew a number of beautiful words having to do with lubricated hydraulic machine parts: DOVETAIL, GOOSENECK, ACORN NUTS and EYEBOLTS. Now I was equally amazed at the poetic names of the stair parts, the beauty of the technical language. NOSING and HAND – so the stair has a body. Whether working with wood or stone, cement or iron: why do humans insist on imposing their face on even the most unwieldy things in the world, why do they name dead matter after their own flesh, personifying it as parts of the body? Is this hidden tenderness necessary to make the harsh work bearable for the technicians? Does every job in every field follow the same principle as my mother's question about the handkerchief?

When I was little we had a handkerchief drawer at home, which was always partitioned into two rows, with three stacks apiece:

On the left the men's handkerchiefs for my father and grandfather.

On the right the women's handkerchiefs for my mother and grandmother.

In the middle the children's handkerchiefs for me.

The drawer was a family portrait in handkerchief format. The men's handkerchiefs were the biggest, with dark stripes along the edges in brown, gray or Bordeaux. The women's handkerchiefs were smaller, and their edges were light blue, red, or green. The children's handkerchiefs were the smallest: borderless white squares painted with flowers or animals. All three handkerchief types were divided into those for everyday use, in the front row, and those reserved for Sunday, in the back. On Sundays your handkerchief had to match the color of your clothes, even if it wasn't visible.

No other object in the house, including ourselves, was ever as important to us as the handkerchief. Its uses were universal: sniffles; nosebleeds; hurt hand, elbow or knee; crying, or biting into it to suppress the crying. A cold wet handkerchief on the forehead for headaches. Tied at the four corners it protected your head against sunburn or rain. If you had to remember something you made a knot to prompt your memory. For carrying heavy bags you wrapped it around your hand. When the train pulled out of the station you waved it to say good-bye. And because the word for tear in our Banat dialect sounds like the Romanian word for train, the squeaking of the railcars on the tracks always sounded to me like crying. In the village if someone died at home they immediately tied a handkerchief around his chin so that his mouth stayed closed when the rigor mortis set in. In the city if a person collapsed on the side of the road, some passerby would always take a handkerchief and cover his face, so that the handkerchief became the dead man's first place of peace.

On hot summer days the parents would send their children to the cemetery late in the evening to water the flowers. We stayed together in groups of two or three, quickly watering one grave and then the next. Afterwards we would huddle together on the steps of the chapel and watch wisps of white mist rise from some of the graves. They would fly up a little ways and disappear in the darkness. For us they were the souls of the dead: animal figures, glasses, little bottles and cups, gloves and stockings. And here and there a white handkerchief bordered by the black night.

Later, when I was meeting with Oskar Pastior so I could write about his deportation to the Soviet labor camp, he told me that an elderly Russian mother had given him a handkerchief made of white batiste. Maybe you will both be lucky, said the Russian woman, and you will come home soon and so will my son. Her son was the same age as Oskar Pastior and as far away from home as he was, but in the opposite direction, she said, in a penal battalion. Oskar Pastior had knocked on her door, a half-starved beggar wanting to trade a lump of coal for a little bit of food. She let him in and gave him some hot soup. And when she saw his nose dripping into the bowl, she gave him the white batiste handkerchief that no one had ever used before. With its a-jour border, and stems and rosettes precisely stitched with silk thread, the handkerchief was a thing of beauty that embraced as well as wounded the beggar. It was a combination: consolation made of batiste, and a silk-stemmed measure of his decrepitude. For the woman, Oskar Pastior was also a combination: an unworldly beggar in her house and a lost child in the world. Both of these personae were delighted and overwhelmed by the gesture of a woman who was two persons for him as well: an unknown Russian woman and the worried mother with the question: DO YOU HAVE A HANDKERCHIEF.

Ever since I heard this story I have had a question of my own: is DO YOU

HAVE A HANDKERCHIEF valid everywhere? Does it stretch halfway across the world in the snowy sheen between freezing and thawing? Does it pass between mountains and steppes to cross every border; can it reach all the way into a gigantic empire strewn with penal and labor camps? Is the question DO YOU HAVE A HANDKERCHIEF impossible to get rid of, even with a hammer and sickle, even with all the camps of Stalinist re-education?

Although I have spoken Romanian for decades, it was only while talking with Oskar Pastior that I realized that the Romanian word for handkerchief is *batistă*. Another example of how sensual the Romanian language is, relentlessly driving its words straight to the heart of things. The material makes no detour, but presents itself ready-made as a handkerchief, as a BATISTĂ. As if all handkerchiefs, whenever and wherever, were made of batiste.

Oskar Pastior kept that handkerchief in his trunk as a reliquary of a double mother with a double son. And after five years of life in the camps he brought it home. Because his white batiste handkerchief was hope and fear. Once you let go of hope and fear, you die.

After our conversation about the white handkerchief I spent half the night pasting up a word collage for Oskar Pastior on a white card:

*Dots are dancing here says Bea*
*you're coming into a long-stemmed glass of milk*
*linens in white gray-green zinc tub*
*nearly all materials*
*correspond upon delivery*
*look here*
*I am the trainride and*
*the cherry in the soapdish*
*never talk to strange men*
*or speak over the switchboard*

When I went to see him later in the week to give him the collage, he said: *you have to paste on FOR OSKAR as well.* I said: *Whatever I give to you is yours.* He said: *You have to paste it on, because the card may not know that.* I took it back home and pasted on: For Oskar. And then I gave it to him the following week, as if I had left the gate first without a handkerchief and now was back the second time with a handkerchief.

Another story also ends with a handkerchief:

My grandparents had a son named Matz. In the 1930s he was sent to study business in Timişoara, so that he could take over the family grain trade and grocery store. The school had teachers from the German Reich, real Nazis. Matz may have been trained as a merchant on the side, but mainly he was taught to be a Nazi – brainwashed according to plan. After he finished, Matz was a passionate Nazi, a changed person. He barked out anti-Semitic slogans, and was as unreachable as an imbecile. My grandfather rebuked him several times: he owed his entire fortune to the credit advanced by Jewish business friends. And when that didn't help, he boxed Matz on the ears several times. But the young man's faculty of reason had been erased. He played the village ideologue, bullying his peers who were dodging the front. Matz had a desk job with the Romanian army. Nevertheless he felt an urge to move from theory to practice, so he volunteered for the SS and asked to be sent to the front. A few months later he came home to marry. Wiser for having seen the crimes at the front, he used a then-current magical formula to escape the war for a few days. The magical formula was called: wedding leave.

My grandmother kept two photos of her son Matz far back in a drawer: a wedding photo and a death photo. The wedding picture shows a bride in white, taller than he by a hand, thin and earnest – a plaster Madonna. On her head was a wreath made of wax that looked like snow-flocked leaves. Next to her was Matz in his Nazi uniform, a soldier instead of a husband, a brideguard instead of a bridegroom. No sooner had he returned to the front, the death photo came. It shows a poor soldier torn to shreds by a mine. The death photo is hand-sized: in the middle of a black field a little gray heap of human remains can be seen resting on a white cloth. Against the black, field the white cloth looks as small as a children's handkerchief, a white square with a strange design painted in the middle. For my grandmother this photo was a combination, too: on the white handkerchief was a dead Nazi, in her memory was a living son. My grandmother kept this double picture inside her prayer book for all her years. She prayed every day, and her prayers almost certainly had double meanings as well. Acknowledging the break from beloved son to fanatic Nazi, they probably beseeched God to perform the balancing act of loving the son and forgiving the Nazi.

My grandfather had been a soldier in the First World War. He knew what he was talking about when he said, often and embittered, in reference to his son Matz: *When the flags start to flutter, common sense slides right into the trumpet.* This warning also applied to the following dictatorship, which I experienced. Every day you could see the common sense of the profiteers, both big and little, sliding right into the trumpet. The trumpet I decided not to blow.

As I child, however, I did have to learn to play the accordion – against my will. Because at home we had the red accordion that had belonged to the dead soldier Matz. The straps were much too long for me. To keep them from slipping off my shoulders, the accordion teacher tied them together on my back with a handkerchief.

Can we say that it is precisely the smallest objects – be they trumpets, accordions, or handkerchiefs – which connect the most disparate things in life? That the objects are in orbit and that their deviations reveal a pattern of repetition – a vicious circle, or what we call in German a devil's circle. We can believe this, but not say it. Still, what can't be said can be written. Because writing is a silent act, a labor from the head to the hand. The mouth is skipped over. I talked a great deal during the dictatorship, mostly because I decided not to blow the trumpet. Usually my talking led to excruciating consequences. But the writing began in silence, there on the stairs, where I had to come to terms with more than could be said. What was happening could no longer be expressed in speech. At most the external accompaniments, but not the totality of the events themselves. That I could only spell out in my head, voicelessly, within the vicious circle of the words during the act of writing. I reacted to the deathly fear with a thirst for life. A hunger for words. Nothing but the whirl of words could grasp my condition. It spelled out what the mouth could not pronounce. I chased after the events, caught up in the words and their devilish circling, until something emerged I had never known before. Parallel to the reality, the pantomime of words stepped into action, without respect for any real dimensions, shrinking what was most important and stretching the minor matters. As it rushes madly ahead, this vicious circle of words imposes a kind of cursed logic on what has been lived. Their pantomime is ruthless and restive, always craving more but instantly jaded. The subject of dictatorship is necessarily present, because nothing can ever again be a matter of course once we have been robbed of nearly all ability to take anything for granted. The subject is there implicitly, but the words are what take possession of me. They coax the subject anywhere they want. Nothing makes sense anymore and everything is true.

When I was a staircase wit, I was as lonely as I had been as a child tending the cows in the river valley. I ate leaves and flowers so I would belong to them, because they knew how to live life and I didn't. I spoke to them by name: *milk thistle* was supposed to mean the prickly plant with milk in its stalk. But the plant didn't listen to the name *milk thistle*. So I tried inventing names with neither *milk* nor *thistle*: THORNRIB, NEEDLENECK. These made-up names uncovered a gap between the plant and me, and the gap opened up into an abyss: the disgrace of talking to myself and not to the plant. But the disgrace was good for me. I looked after the cows and the sound of the words looked after me. I felt:

*Every word in your face,*
*Knows something of the vicious circle*
*But doesn't say it*

The sound of the words knows that it has no choice but to beguile, because objects deceive with their materials, and feelings mislead with their gestures. The sound of the words, along with the truth this sound invents, resides at the interface, where the deceit of the materials and that of the gestures come together. In writing, it is not a matter of trusting, but rather of the honesty of the deceit.

Back then in the factory, when I was a staircase wit and the handkerchief was my office, I also looked up the beautiful word TREPPENZINS or ASCENDING INTEREST RATE, when the interest rate for a loan ascends as if climbing a stair. (In German this is called "Stair Interest.") These ascending rates are costs for one person and income for another. In writing they become both, the deeper I delve into the text. The more that which is written takes from me, the more it shows what was missing from the experience that was lived. Only the words make this discovery, because they didn't know it earlier. And where they catch the lived experience by surprise is where they reflect it best. In the end they become so compelling that the lived experience must cling to them in order not to fall apart.

It seems to me that the objects don't know their material, the gestures don't know their feelings, and the words don't know the mouth that speaks them. But to be certain of our own existence, we need the objects, the gestures, and the words. After all, the more words we are allowed to take, the freer we become. If our mouth is banned, then we attempt to assert ourselves through gestures, even objects. They are more difficult to interpret, and take time before they arouse suspicion. They can help us turn humiliation into a type of dignity that takes time to arouse suspicion.

Early one morning, shortly before I emigrated from Romania, a village policeman came for my mother. She was already at the gate, when it occurred to her: DO YOU HAVE A HANDKERCHIEF. She didn't. Even though the policeman was impatient, she went back inside to get a handkerchief. At the station the policeman flew into a rage. My mother's Romanian was too limited to understand his screaming. So he left the office and bolted the door from the outside. My mother sat there locked up the whole day. The first hours she sat on his desk and cried. Then she paced up and down and began using the handkerchief that was wet with her tears to dust the furniture. After that she took the water bucket out of the corner and the towel off the hook on the wall and mopped the floor. I was horrified when she told me. *How can you clean the office for him like that* I asked. She said, without embarrassment: *I was looking for some work to pass the time. And the office was so dirty. Good thing I took one of the large men's handkerchiefs with me.*

Only then did I understand that through this additional, but voluntary humiliation, she had created some dignity for herself in her detention. I tried to find the words for it in a collage:

*I thought about the sturdy rose in my heart*
*about the useless soul like a sieve*
*but the keeper asked:*
*who will gain the upper hand*
*I said: saving the skin*
*he shouted: the skin is*
*nothing but a scrap of insulted batiste*
*with no common sense*

I wish I could utter a sentence for all those whom dictatorships deprive of dignity every day, up to and including the present – a sentence, perhaps, containing the word handkerchief. Or else the question: DO YOU HAVE A HANDKERCHIEF?

Can it be that the question about the handkerchief was never about the handkerchief at all, but rather about the acute solitude of a human being?

Translated by Philip Boehm

Portrait photo of Ms. Müller by photographer Ulla Montan.

Literature 2010

**Mario Vargas Llosa**

*"for his cartography of structures of power and his trenchant images of the individual's resistance, revolt, and defeat"*

# THE NOBEL PRIZE IN LITERATURE

Speech by Writer Per Wästberg of the Swedish Academy.
Translation of the Swedish text.

*Your Majesties, Your Royal Highnesses, Esteemed Laureates, Ladies and Gentlemen,*

Mario Vargas Llosa's writing has shaped our image of South America and has its own chapter in the history of contemporary literature. In his early years, he was a renewer of the novel; today, an epic poet of not only Latin American stature. His wide embrace enfolds all literary genres.

He is hard to classify. From the provincial city of Arequipa in Peru emerged: a citizen of the world, a Marxist transformed by Castro's misdeeds into a liberal, a losing presidential candidate later to appear on his country's postage stamps, an epic poet and historian, a satirist, an eroticist, an essayist and columnist addressing most issues – including football and fear of flying. As a reporter from the world's flashpoints, he recalls Graham Greene.

Vargas Llosa has led us through unfamiliar milieux with an authority that lends the authenticity of a 19th-century explorer. He links the narrative tradition of Balzac and Tolstoy to the modernistic experiments of William Faulkner.

Rebellion against an authoritarian father sparked an opposition against circumstance that extended into a youthful escape to literature and imagination. The rebel remains his protagonist – also in the forms of Flora Tristan and her grandson Paul Gauguin, fighting the conventions of their times, or the Irishman Roger Casement who, in a new novel by Vargas Llosa, exposes slavery in the Congo of Leopold II. *Nota bene,* revolt is successful only as narrative; as long as tyrannical fathers exist in our lives and societies, revolt remains permanent.

Vargas Llosa uses fiction to penetrate the shrouds of power and explore the obsessions of its exploiters. The halls of boarding schools and the corridors of administrations stand against indomitable open-air inhabitants, though the latter seldom triumph in defying regulation and imposition. History crushes Vargas Llosa's figures but not their consciences.

In Latin America, writers are charged with the moral duty of not collaborating in injustice. But the demand for commitment can cripple desire and imagination. Vargas Llosa's novels never bow to diktat; they are polyphonic and open to interpretation, emphasising the diversity of Latin America's social and ethnic patterns. He lends voice to the silenced and oppressed – an aesthetic feat and an ethical act. He has an unreserved interest in people – from presidents to prostitutes – and nothing is alien to him, from the arrogance of statesmen to love's subtlest plots.

In his dark picaresque, *The War of the End of the World,* Vargas Llosa is fascinated by fanatics and their world vision. A prophet foresees the end of the world in 1900 and assembles an army of shabby misfits that frustrates Brazil's military forces. Another fanatic, *Mayta in The Real Life of Alejandro Mayta,* is an Indian quadroon in an underground leftwing sect, first idealist, then terrorist in a Peru on the brink of disintegration. It is a confrontation with youthful revolutionary romanticism. And it is to the mire of social and political chasms that Vargas Llosa has led us, with serene linguistic agility, ever since his early novels, *The Time of the Hero and The Green House.*

Vargas Llosa's late novel about the abuse of power, *The Feast of the Goat,* depicts the Dominican Republic's tyrant, Trujillo. Servility and despotism are portrayed with brutal intensity, the horrors balanced by compassion and humanity. Among the bizarre detail is the revelation that the dictator coerced the country's poets into petitioning the Swedish Academy to award his scarcely learned wife the Nobel Prize in Literature.

Vargas Llosa has an eye for the foolishness of innocence and the lethargy of evil. He is unusual in his ability to depict men's friendship as well as sadistic penalism and hierarchical vanity. He prefers the compromises of common sense to radical utopias. In his book about Flaubert, Vargas Llosa disarmingly claims that he and Emma Bovary have in common "our taste for pleasures of the flesh rather than of the soul, our respect for senses and instincts, our preference for this earthly life above all else".

He writes of love and its absence, of the seduction of violence and the rare triumph of justice. In his erotic entertainments he is a playful ruffian unafraid of self-mockery. Or, as he expressed it: "There is no great art without a measure of folly, since great art expresses the entirety of human experience, where intuition, obsession, madness and fantasy play their part just as ideas do." Vargas Llosa believes in the force of literature. Without literature there would be no rendition of mankind's possibilities and hidden places. It is a bulwark against prejudice, racism and intolerant nationalism, since in all great literature, men and women of the entire world are equally alive. It is harder to suppress a people that reads a lot.

So he has fought for freedom of expression and for human rights regardless of geography, and has done so with a passion for liberty and with political courage and common sense – these not always in harmony in important writers. In a time of tiresome narcissism he is what Zola, André Gide and Camus embodied: an example and a bellwether.

¡Estimado Mario Vargas Llosa!

Usted ha encapsulado la historia de la sociedad del siglo veinte en una burbuja de imaginación. Ésta se ha mantenido flotando en el aire durante cincuenta años y todavía reluce. La Academia sueca le felicita. ¡Acérquese y reciba el premio Nobel de literatura de este año de la mano de su Majestad el Rey!

'My dear Mario Vargas Llosa,

You have encapsulated 20th-century history in a bubble of imagination. It has floated on air for 50 years and shines still. The Swedish Academy congratulates you. Please step forward to receive this year's Nobel Prize in Literature from the hands of His Majesty the King.'

# MARIO VARGAS LLOSA

Mario Vargas Llosa was born in 1936 in Arequipa, Peru's second largest city. During his childhood in Cochabamba, Bolivia, and Piura, a city in the north of Peru, he believed that his father had died. However, this was a lie told by his mother to conceal their tortuous separation. The truth emerged when, in 1946, his father appeared unexpectedly to take him away from his mother's parents, moving with him and his mother to Lima. This revelation signified an abrupt change in Vargas Llosa's life, from the pampered upbringing of a feminine environment to the hostile treatment of an authoritarian father. At his side, he was to discover fear, injustice and violence for the first time.

During these years in which he left his childhood behind, devouring the works of Dumas and Victor Hugo, the political climate in Peru was a reflection of Vargas Llosa's home life. The dictator Manuel Odría rose to power in 1948 and over the next eight years, while Vargas Llosa studied law and literature at the University of San Marcos, he imposed rigid controls on social life which stifled individuality, engendering scepticism, defeatism and frustration among Peruvians. This period later inspired his novel *Conversation in the Cathedral*, published in 1969.

The dominant presence of authoritarianism in both public and private spheres led Vargas Llosa to strongly condemn systems which, in one way or another, sought to inhibit individual initiative and restrict personal freedom. His literary works, starting with *The Time of the Hero* (1963) – one of the key novels which pioneered the 'Boom' period in Latin American literature – reflect his loathing of arbitrary manifestations of power and the absence of law which enables the strongest to impose their will. The inspiration for this novel was the time he spent between 1950 and 1951 in the Leoncio Prado Military Academy, where he was sent by his father to stifle his literary ambitions through military discipline. However, Vargas Llosa managed to rebel against his paternal yoke, not only pursuing a writing career, but also marrying his maternal uncle's sister-in-law Julia Urquidi, who was eleven years older than him and divorced. He drew on these experiences to write his novel *Aunt Julia and the Scriptwriter*, published in 1977.

Another fundamental experience in his life was a journey he made in the Amazon jungle in 1958, which inspired novels such as *The Green House* (1966), *Captain Pantoja and the Special Service* (1973), *The Storyteller* (1987) and *The Dream of the Celt* (2010). As opposed to other city dwellers who first came into contact with the remote jungle landscapes of Peru, which are still inhabited by primitive indigenous tribes, Vargas Llosa found neither exoticism nor harmony between humanity and nature but rather despotism, violence and cruelty. The absence of law and institutions exposed the jungle natives to the worst humiliations and acts of injustice by colonists, missionaries and adventurers, who had come to impose their will through the use of terror and force. What he heard, saw and felt in the jungle convinced Vargas Llosa that the archaic Peru which survived in the depths of the Amazon and the peaks of the Andes should be integrated into a modern Peru, the only Peru which, due to its legal framework, could stop the pillaging and wrongful acts committed against minorities and the most vulnerable sectors of Peruvian society.

Until the early seventies, Vargas Llosa perceived in socialism and the Cuban revolution a series of ideas which embodied modernity and a solution to the moral vices and economic underdevelopment of Latin America. However, when the revolution showed signs of having become an oppressive dictatorship where writers felt their freedom to create was restricted, Vargas Llosa distanced himself from Fidel Castro and socialism and began to advocate reformism, liberal pluralism, democracy and the free market. His changing political inclination brought with it a new way of understanding Latin American problems. The revolution, the dictatorship, nationalism, racism and religious mysticism, all of which are present throughout the course of the republican history of Latin America, now proved to be symptoms of a deeper problem related to intolerance and dogmatism. A host of leaders, rebels and saviours had instigated fanatical attempts to impose a closed view of the world with no concern for the consequences. This human tendency, which is ever present in Latin America and the root cause behind innumerable tragedies, provided the plot for his novel *The War of the End of the World* in 1981.

In 1987 the attempt by the then president of Peru, Alan García, to nationalise the banking industry was vehemently rejected by Vargas Llosa, who saw this project as a strategy to accumulate power and place the media and businesses in government hands. With the support of large sectors of the population, Vargas Llosa organised protest marches which catapulted him into the political arena. His *Movimiento Libertad,* which opposed Alan García, evolved into the *Frente Democrático,* three years later. As the leader of this party he ran in the presidential elections in 1990. However, he lost in the second round to the engineer Alberto Fujimori, who then shut down congress and established a despotic and corrupt dictatorship for which he is currently serving a sentence. Memories of these years can be found in his book of memoirs *A Fish in the Water* (1993).

Since 1990 Vargas Llosa has published a fortnightly column in the Spanish daily newspaper *El País,* which is reprinted in different media sources all over the world. In these, he states his opinion regarding the most important current political, social and cultural events. He also teaches literature courses at American universities and writes literary essays. Although Vargas Llosa began writing plays in the 1980s, it was not until 2005 that he decided to take to the stage himself to portray his characters. Aitana Sánchez Gijón, the actress who accompanies him in this new adventure, has described him as a promising young actor.

Translated by Colin Howe

# IN PRAISE OF READING AND FICTION

Nobel Lecture, December 7, 2010

by

MARIO VARGAS LLOSA

Lima, Peru.

I learned to read at the age of five, in Brother Justiniano's class at the De la Salle Academy in Cochabamba, Bolivia. It is the most important thing that has ever happened to me. Almost seventy years later I remember clearly how the magic of translating the words in books into images enriched my life, breaking the barriers of time and space and allowing me to travel with Captain Nemo twenty thousand leagues under the sea, fight with d'Artagnan, Athos, Portos, and Aramis against the intrigues threatening the Queen in the days of the secretive Richelieu, or stumble through the sewers of Paris, transformed into Jean Valjean carrying Marius's inert body on my back.

Reading changed dreams into life and life into dreams and placed the universe of literature within reach of the boy I once was. My mother told me the first things I wrote were continuations of the stories I read because it made me sad when they concluded or because I wanted to change their endings. And perhaps this is what I have spent my life doing without realising it: prolonging in time, as I grew, matured, and aged, the stories that filled my childhood with exaltation and adventures.

I wish my mother were here, a woman who was moved to tears reading the poems of Amado Nervo and Pablo Neruda, and Grandfather Pedro too, with his large nose and gleaming bald head, who celebrated my verses, and Uncle Lucho, who urged me so energetically to throw myself body and soul into writing even though literature, in that time and place, compensated its devotees so badly. Throughout my life I have had people like that at my side, people who loved and encouraged me and infected me with their faith when I had doubts. Thanks to them, and certainly to my obstinacy and some luck, I have been able to devote most of my time to the passion, the vice, the marvel of writing, creating a parallel life where we can take refuge against adversity, one that makes the extraordinary natural and the natural extraordinary, that dissipates chaos, beautifies ugliness, eternalises the moment, and turns death into a passing spectacle.

Writing stories was not easy. When they were turned into words, projects withered on the paper and ideas and images failed. How to reanimate them? Fortunately, the masters were there, teachers to learn from and examples to follow. Flaubert taught me that talent is unyielding discipline and long patience. Faulkner, that form – writing and structure – elevates or impoverishes subjects. Martorell, Cervantes, Dickens, Balzac, Tolstoy, Conrad, Thomas Mann, that scope and ambition are as important in a novel as stylistic dexterity and narrative strategy. Sartre, that words are acts, that a novel, a play, or an essay, engaged with the present moment and better options, can change the course of history. Camus and Orwell, that a literature stripped of morality is inhuman, and Malraux that heroism and the epic are as possible in the present as is the time of the Argonauts, the *Odyssey*, and the *Iliad.*

If in this address I were to summon all the writers to whom I owe a few things or a great deal, their shadows would plunge us into darkness. They are innumerable. In addition to revealing the secrets of the storytelling craft, they obliged me to explore the bottomless depths of humanity, admire its heroic deeds, and feel horror at its savagery. They were my most obliging friends, the ones who vitalised my calling and in whose books I discovered that there is hope even in the worst of circumstances, that living is worth the effort if only because without life we could not read or imagine stories.

At times I wondered whether writing was not a solipsistic luxury in countries like mine, where there were scant readers, so many people who were poor and illiterate, so much injustice, and where culture was a privilege of the few. These doubts, however, never stifled my calling, and I always kept writing even during those periods when earning a living absorbed most of my time. I believe I did the right thing, since if, for literature to flourish, it was first necessary for a society to achieve high culture, freedom, prosperity, and justice, it never would have existed. But thanks to literature, to the consciousness it shapes, the desires and longings it inspires, and our disenchantment with reality when we return from the journey to a beautiful fantasy, civilisation is now less cruel than when storytellers began to humanise life with their fables. We would be worse than we are without the good books we have read, more conformist, not as restless, more submissive, and the critical spirit, the engine of progress, would not even exist. Like writing, reading is a protest against the insufficiencies of life. When we look in fiction for what is missing in life, we are saying, with no need to say it or even to know it, that life as it is does not satisfy our thirst for the absolute – the foundation of the human condition – and should be better. We invent fictions in order to live somehow the many lives we would like to lead when we barely have one at our disposal.

Without fictions we would be less aware of the importance of freedom for life to be liveable, the hell it turns into when it is trampled underfoot by a tyrant, an ideology or a religion. Let those who doubt that literature not only submerges us in the dream of beauty and happiness but alerts us to every kind of oppression, ask themselves why all regimes determined to control the behaviour of citizens from cradle to grave fear it so much they establish systems of censorship to repress it and keep so wary an eye on independent writers. They do this because they know the risk of allowing the imagination to wander free in books, know how seditious fictions become when the reader compares the freedom that makes them possible and is exercised in them with the obscurantism and fear lying in wait in the real world. Whether they want it or not, know it or not, when they invent stories the writers of tales propagate dissatisfaction, demonstrating that the world is badly made and the life of fantasy richer than the life of our daily routine. This fact, if it takes root in their sensibility and consciousness, makes citizens more difficult to manipulate, less willing to accept the lies of the interrogators and jailers who would like to make them believe that behind bars they lead more secure and better lives.

Good literature erects bridges between different peoples, and by having us enjoy, suffer, or feel surprise, unites us beneath the languages, beliefs, habits, customs, and prejudices that separate us. When the great white whale buries Captain Ahab in the sea, the hearts of readers take fright in exactly the same way in Tokyo, Lima, or Timbuktu. When Emma Bovary swallows arsenic, Anna Karenina throws herself in front of the train, and Julien Sorel climbs to the scaffold, and when, in "El sur," the urban doctor Juan Dahlmann walks out of that tavern on the pampa to face a thug's knife, or we realise that all the residents of Comala, Pedro Páramo's village, are dead, the shudder is the same in the reader who worships Buddha, Confucius, Christ, Allah, or is an agnostic, wears a jacket and tie, a jalaba, a kimono or bombachas. Literature creates a fraternity within human diversity and eclipses the frontiers erected among men and women by ignorance, ideologies, religions, languages and stupidity.

Since every period has its horrors, ours is the age of fanatics, of suicide terrorists, an ancient species convinced that by killing they earn heaven, that the blood of innocents washes away collective affronts, corrects injustices, and imposes truth on false beliefs. Every day, all over the world, countless victims are sacrificed by those who feel they possess absolute truths. With the collapse of totalitarian empires, we believed that living together, peace, pluralism, and human rights would gain the ascendancy and the world would leave behind holocausts, genocides, invasions and wars of extermination. None of that has occurred. New forms of barbarism flourish, incited by fanaticism, and with the proliferation of weapons of mass destruction, we cannot overlook the fact that any small faction of crazed redeemers may one day provoke a nuclear cataclysm. We have to thwart them, confront them and defeat them. There aren't many, although the tumult of their crimes resounds all over the planet and the nightmares they provoke overwhelm us with dread. We should not allow ourselves to be intimidated by those who want to snatch away the freedom we have been acquiring over the long course of civilisation. Let us defend the liberal democracy that, with all its limitations, continues to signify political pluralism, coexistence, tolerance, human rights, respect for criticism, legality, free elections, alternation in power, everything that has been taking us out of a savage life and bringing us closer – though we will never attain it – to the beautiful, perfect life literature devises, the one we can deserve only by inventing, writing, and reading it. By confronting homicidal fanatics we defend our right to dream and to make our dreams reality.

In my youth, like many writers of my generation, I was a Marxist and believed socialism would be the remedy for the exploitation and social injustices that were becoming more severe in my country, in Latin America and in the rest of the Third World. My disillusion with statism and collectivism and my transition to the democrat and liberal that I am – that I try to be – was long and difficult and carried out slowly as a consequence of episodes like the conversion of the Cuban Revolution, about which I initially had been enthusiastic, to the authoritarian, vertical model of the Soviet Union; the testimony of dissidents who managed to slip past the barbed wire fences of the Gulag; the invasion of Czechoslovakia by the nations of the Warsaw Pact; and because of thinkers like Raymond Aron, Jean Francois Révei, Isaiah Berlin and Karl Popper, to whom I owe my re-evaluation of democratic culture and open societies. Those masters were an example of lucidity and gallant courage when the intelligentsia of the West, as a result of frivolity or opportunism, appeared to have succumbed to the spell of Soviet socialism or, even worse, to the bloody witches' Sabbath of the Chinese Cultural Revolution.

As a boy I dreamed of coming some day to Paris because, dazzled by French literature, I believed that living there and breathing the air breathed by Balzac, Stendhal, Baudelaire and Proust would help transform me into a real writer, and if I did not leave Peru I would be only a pseudo Sundays-and-holidays writer. And the truth is I owe to France and French culture unforgettable lessons, for example that literature is as much a calling as it is a discipline, a job, an obstinacy. I lived there when Sartre and Camus were alive and writing, in the years of Ionesco, Beckett, Bataille, and Cioran, the discovery of the theatre of Brecht and the films of Ingmar Bergman, the Theatre National Populaire of Jean Vilar and the Odéon of Jean-Louis Barrault, of the Nouvelle Vague and the Nouveau Roman and the speeches, beautiful literary pieces, of André Malraux, and what may have been the most theatrical spectacle in Europe during that time, the press conferences and Olympic thunderings of General de Gaulle. But perhaps I am most grateful to France for the discovery of Latin America. There I learned that Peru was part of a vast community united by history, geography, social and political problems, a certain mode of being, and the delicious language it spoke and wrote. And in those same years, it was producing a new, forceful literature. There I read Borges, Octavio Paz, Cortázar, García Márquez, Fuentes, Cabrera Infante, Rulfo, Onetti, Carpentier, Edwards, Donoso and many others whose writings were revolutionising narrative in the Spanish language, and thanks to whom Europe and a good part of the world discovered that Latin America was not the continent only of coups, operetta despots, bearded guerrillas and the maracas of the mambo and the cha-cha-cha but of ideas, artistic forms and literary fantasies that transcended the picturesque and spoke a universal language.

From that time to this, not without stumbling and blunders, Latin America has made progress although, as César Vallejo said in a poem, *Hay, hermanos, muchísimo que hacer* [There is still, brothers, so much to do]. We are afflicted with fewer dictatorships than before, only Cuba and her named successor, Venezuela, and some pseudo populist, clownish democracies like those in Bolivia and Nicaragua. But in the rest of the continent democracy is functioning, supported by a broad popular consensus, and for the first time in our history, as in Brazil, Chile, Uruguay, Peru, Colombia, the Dominican Republic, Mexico, and almost all of Central America, we have a left and a right that respect legality, the freedom to criticise, elections and succession in power. That is the right road, and if it stays on it, combats insidious corruption, and continues to integrate with the world, Latin America will finally stop being the continent of the future and become the continent of the present.

I never felt like a foreigner in Europe or, in fact, anywhere. In all the places I have lived, in Paris, London, Barcelona, Madrid, Berlin, Washington, New York, Brazil or the Dominican Republic, I felt at home. I have always found a lair where I could live in peace, work, learn things, nurture dreams, and find friends, good books to read and subjects to write about. It does not seem to me that my unintentionally becoming a citizen of the world has weakened what are called "my roots," my connections to my own country – which would not be particularly important – because if that were so, my Peruvian experiences would not continue to nourish me as a writer and would not always appear in my stories, even when they seem to occur very far from Peru. I believe instead that living for so long outside the country where I was born has strengthened those connections, adding a more lucid perspective to them, and a nostalgia that can differentiate the adjectival from the substantive and keep memories reverberating. Love of the country where one was born cannot be obligatory, but like any other love must be a spontaneous act of the heart, like the one that unites lovers, parents and children and friends.

I carry Peru deep inside me because that is where I was born, grew up, was formed, and lived those experiences of childhood and youth that shaped my personality and forged my calling, and there I loved, hated, enjoyed, suffered and dreamed. What happens there affects me more, moves and exasperates me more than what occurs elsewhere. I have not wished it or imposed it on myself; it simply is so. Some compatriots accused me of being a traitor, and I was on the verge of losing my citizenship when, during the last dictatorship, I asked the democratic governments of the world to penalise the regime with diplomatic and economic sanctions, as I have always done with all dictatorships of any kind, whether of Pinochet, Fidel Castro, the Taliban in Afghanistan, the Imams in Iran, apartheid in South Africa, the uniformed satraps of Burma (now called Myanmar). And I would do it again tomorrow if – may destiny not wish it and Peruvians not permit it – Peru were once again the victim of a coup that would annihilate our fragile democracy. It was not the precipitate, emotional action of a resentful man, as some scribblers wrote, accustomed to judging others from the point of view of their own pettiness. It was an act in line with my conviction that a dictatorship represents absolute evil for a country, a source of brutality and corruption and profound wounds that take a long time to close, poison the nation's future and create pernicious habits and practices that endure for generations and delay democratic reconstruction. This is why dictatorships must be fought without hesitation, with all the means at our disposal, including economic sanctions. It is regrettable that democratic governments, instead of setting an example by making common cause with those, like the Damas de Blanco in Cuba, the Venezuelan opposition, or Aung San Suu Kyi and Liu Xiaobo, who courageously confront the dictatorships they endure, often show themselves complaisant not with them but with their tormenters. Those valiant people, struggling for their freedom, are also struggling for ours.

A compatriot of mine, José María Arguedas, called Peru the country of "every blood." I do not believe any formula defines it better: that is what we are and that is what all Peruvians carry inside us, whether we like it or not: an aggregate of traditions, races, beliefs and cultures proceeding from the four cardinal points. I am proud to feel myself the heir to the pre-Hispanic cultures that created the textiles and feather mantles of Nazca and Paracas and the Mochican or Incan ceramics exhibited in the best museums in the world, the builders of Machu Picchu, Gran Chimú, Chan Chan, Kuelap, Sipán, the burial grounds of La Bruja and El Sol and La Luna, and to the Spaniards who, with their saddle bags, swords, and horses, brought to Peru Greece, Rome, the Judeo-Christian tradition, the Renaissance, Cervantes, Quevedo, and Góngora and the harsh language of Castile sweetened by the Andes. And with Spain came Africa, with its strength, its music, and its effervescent imagination, to enrich Peruvian heterogeneity. If we investigate only a little we discover that Peru, like the Aleph of Borges, is a small format of the entire world. What an extraordinary privilege for a country not to have an identity because it has all of them!

The conquest of America was cruel and violent, like all conquests, of course, and we should criticise it but not forget as we do that those who committed pillage and crimes were, for the most part, our great-grandfathers and great-great-grandfathers, the Spaniards who came to America and adopted American ways, not those who remained in their own country. Such criticism, to be just, should be self-criticism. Because when we gained our independence from Spain two hundred years ago, those who assumed power in the former colonies, instead of liberating the Indians and creating justice for old wrongs, continued to exploit them with as much greed and ferocity as the conquerors and, in some countries, decimating and exterminating them. Let us say this with absolute clarity: for two centuries the emancipation of the indigenous population has been our exclusive responsibility, and we have not fulfilled it. This continues to be an unresolved issue in all of Latin America. There is not a single exception to this ignominy and shame.

I love Spain as much as Peru, and my debt to her is as great as my gratitude. If not for Spain, I never would have reached this podium or become a known writer and perhaps, like so many unfortunate colleagues, I would wander in the limbo of writers without luck, publishers, prizes or readers, whose talent – sad comfort – posterity may one day discover. All my books were published in Spain, where I received exaggerated recognition, and friends like Carlos

Barral, Carmen Balcells, and so many others were zealous about my stories having readers. And Spain granted me a second nationality when I could have lost mine. I have never felt the slightest incompatibility between being Peruvian and having a Spanish passport, because I have always felt that Spain and Peru are two sides of the same coin, not only in my small person but in essential realities like history, language and culture.

Of all the years I have lived on Spanish soil, I remember as most brilliant the five I spent in a dearly loved Barcelona in the early 1970s. Franco's dictatorship was still in power and shooting, but by then it was a fossil in rags, and especially in the field of culture, incapable of maintaining its earlier controls. Cracks and chinks were opening that the censors could not patch over, and through them Spanish society absorbed new ideas, books, currents of thought, and artistic values and forms prohibited until then as subversive. No city took as much or better advantage of this start of an opening than Barcelona or experienced a comparable excitement in all fields of ideas and creativity. It became the cultural capital of Spain, the place you had to be to breathe anticipation of the freedom to come. And, in a sense, it was also the cultural capital of Latin America because of the number of painters, writers, publishers, and artists from Latin American countries who either settled in or travelled back and forth to Barcelona: it was where you had to be if you wanted to be a poet, novelist, painter or composer in our time. For me, those were unforgettable years of comradeship, friendship, plots and fertile intellectual work. Just as Paris had been, Barcelona was a Tower of Babel, a cosmopolitan, universal city where it was stimulating to live and work and where, for the first time since the days of the Civil War, Spanish and Latin American writers mixed and fraternised, recognising one another as possessors of the same tradition and allied in a common enterprise and certainty: the end of the dictatorship was imminent and in democratic Spain, culture would be the principal protagonist.

Although it did not occur exactly that way, the Spanish transition from dictatorship to democracy has been one of the best stories of modern times, an example of how, when good sense and reason prevail and political adversaries set aside sectarianism for the common good, events can occur as marvellous as the ones in novels of magic realism. The Spanish transition from authoritarianism to freedom, from underdevelopment to prosperity, from third-world economic contrasts and inequalities to a country of middle classes, her integration into Europe and her adoption in a few years of a democratic culture, has astonished the entire world and precipitated Spain's modernisation. It has been moving and instructive for me to experience this near at hand, at times from the inside. I fervently hope that nationalism, the incurable plague of the modern world and of Spain as well, does not ruin this happy tale.

I despise every form of nationalism, a provincial ideology – or rather, religion – that is short-sighted, exclusive, that cuts off the intellectual horizon and hides in its bosom ethnic and racist prejudices, for it transforms into a supreme value, a moral and ontological privilege, the fortuitous circumstance of one's birthplace. Along with religion, nationalism has been the cause of the worst slaughters in history, like those in the two world wars and the current bloodletting in the Middle East. Nothing has contributed as much as nationalism to Latin America's having been Balkanised and stained with blood in senseless battles and disputes, squandering astronomical resources to purchase weapons instead of building schools, libraries and hospitals.

We should not confuse a blinkered nationalism and its rejection of the "other," always the seed of violence, with patriotism, a salutary, generous feeling of love for the land where we were born, where our ancestors lived, where our first dreams were forged, a familiar landscape of geographies, loved ones and events that are transformed into signposts of memory and defences against solitude. Homeland is not flags, anthems or apodictic speeches about emblematic heroes, but a handful of places and people that populate our memories and tinge them with melancholy, the warm sensation that no matter where we are, there is a home for us to return to.

Peru is for me Arequipa, where I was born but never lived, a city my mother, grandparents, and aunts and uncles taught me to know through their memories and yearnings, because my entire family tribe, as Arequepeños tend to do, always carried the White City with them in their wandering existence. It is Piura in the desert, mesquite trees and the long-suffering burros that Piurans of my youth called "somebody else's feet" – an elegant, sad name – where I discovered that storks did not bring babies into the world but couples made them by doing outrageous things that were a mortal sin. It is San Miguel Academy and the Varieties Theatre where for the first time I saw a short work I had written produced on stage. It is the corner of Diego Ferré and Colón, in Lima's Miraflores – we called it the Happy Neighborhood – where I exchanged short pants for long trousers, smoked my first cigarette, learned to dance, fall in love, and open my heart to girls. It is the dusty, pulsing editorial offices of the paper *La Crónica* where, at sixteen, I stood virgil over my first arms as a journalist, a trade that, along with literature, has occupied almost my entire life and, like books, has made me live more, know the world better, and be with men and women from everywhere and every class, excellent, good, bad and execrable people. It is the Leoncio Prado Military Academy, where I learned that Peru was not the small middle-class redoubt where I had lived until then, confined and protected, but a large, ancient, rancorous, unequal country, shaken by all kinds of social storms. It is the clandestine cells of Cahuide where, with a handful of San Marcos students, we prepared the world revolution. And Peru is my friends in the Freedom Movement with whom for three years, in the midst of bombs, blackouts and terrorist assassinations, we worked in defence of democracy and the culture of freedom.

Peru is Patricia, my cousin with the upturned nose and indomitable character, whom I was lucky enough to marry forty-five years ago and who still endures the manias, neuroses and temper tantrums that help me to write. Without her my life would have dissolved a long time ago into a turbulent whirlwind, and Alvaro, Gonzalo, Morgana and the six grandchildren who extend and gladden our existence would not have been born. She does everything and does everything well. She solves problems, manages the economy, imposes order on chaos, keeps journalists and intrusive people at bay, defends my time, decides appointments and trips, packs and unpacks suitcases, and is so generous that even when she thinks she is rebuking me, she pays me the highest compliment: "Mario, the only thing you're good for is writing."

Let us return to literature. The paradise of childhood is not a literary myth for me but a reality I lived and enjoyed in the large family house with three courtyards in Cochabamba, where with my cousins and school friends we could reproduce the stories of Tarzan and Salgari, and in the prefecture of Piura, where bats nested in the lofts, silent shadows that filled the starry nights of that hot land with mystery. During those years, writing was playing a game my family celebrated, something charming that earned applause for me, the grandson, the nephew, the son without a papa because my father had died and gone to heaven. He was a tall, good-looking man in a navy uniform whose photo adorned my night table, which I prayed to and then kissed before going to sleep. One Piuran morning – I do not think I have recovered from it yet – my mother revealed that the gentleman was, in fact, alive. And on that very day we were going to live with him in Lima. I was eleven years old, and from that moment everything changed. I lost my innocence and discovered loneliness, authority, adult life and fear. My salvation was reading, reading good books, taking refuge in those worlds where life was glorious, intense, one adventure after another, where I could feel free and be happy again. And it was writing, in secret, like someone giving himself up to an unspeakable vice, a forbidden passion. Literature stopped being a game. It became a way of resisting adversity, protesting, rebelling, escaping the intolerable, my reason for living. From then until now, in every circumstance when I have felt disheartened or beaten down, on the edge of despair, giving myself body and soul to my work as a storyteller has been the light at the end of the tunnel, the plank that carries the shipwrecked man to shore.

Although it is very difficult and forces me to sweat blood and, like every writer, to feel at times the threat of paralysis, a dry season of the imagination, nothing has made me enjoy life as much as spending months and years constructing a story, from its uncertain beginnings, the image memory stores of a lived experience that becomes a restlessness, an enthusiasm, a daydream that then germinates into a project and the decision to attempt to convert the agitated cloud of phantoms into a story. "Writing is a way of living," said Flaubert. Yes, absolutely, a way of living with illusion and joy and a fire throwing out sparks in your head, struggling with intractable words until you master them, exploring the broad world like a hunter tracking down desirable prey to feed an embryonic fiction and appease the voracious appetite of every story that, as it grows, would like to devour every other story. Beginning to feel the vertigo a gestating novel leads us to, when it takes shape and seems to begin to live on its own, with characters that move, act, think, feel, and demand respect and consideration, on whom it is no longer possible to arbitrarily impose behaviour or to deprive them of their free will without killing them, without having the story lose its power to persuade – this is an experience that continues to bewitch me as it did the first time, as complete and dizzying as making love to the woman you love for days, weeks, months, without stopping.

When speaking of fiction, I have talked a great deal about the novel and very little about the theatre, another of its pre-eminent forms. A great injustice, of course. Theatre was my first love, ever since, as an adolescent, I saw Arthur Miller's *Death of a Salesman* at the Segura Theatre in Lima, a performance that left me transfixed with emotion and precipitated my writing a drama with Incas. If there had been a theatrical movement in the Lima of the 1950s, I would have been a playwright rather than a novelist. There was not, and that must have turned me more and more toward narrative. But my love for the theatre never ended; it dozed, curled up in the shadow of novels, like a temptation and a nostalgia, above all whenever I saw an enthralling play. In the late 1970s, the persistent memory of a hundred-year-old great-aunt, Mamaé, who in the final years of her life cut off her surrounding reality to take refuge in memories and fiction, suggested a story. And I felt, prophetically, that it was a story for the theatre, that only on stage would it take on the animation and splendour of successful fictions. I wrote it with the tremulous excitement of a beginner and so enjoyed seeing it on stage with Norma Aleandro in the heroine's role that since then, between novels and essays, I have relapsed several times. And I must add, I never imagined that at the age of seventy I would mount (I should say, stumble onto) a stage to act. That reckless adventure made me experience for the first time in my own flesh and bone the miracle it is for someone who has spent his life writing fictions to embody for a few hours a character of fantasy, to live the fiction in front of an audience. I can never adequately thank my dear friends, the director Joan Ollé and the actress Aitana Sánchez Gijón, for having encouraged me to share with them that fantastic experience (in spite of the panic that accompanied it).

Literature is a false representation of life that nevertheless helps us to understand life better, to orient ourselves in the labyrinth where we are born, pass by and die. It compensates for the reverses and frustrations real life inflicts on us, and because of it we can decipher, at least partially, the hieroglyphic that existence tends to be for the great majority of human beings, principally those of us who generate more doubts than certainties and confess our perplexity before subjects like transcendence, individual and collective destiny, the soul, the sense or senselessness of history, the to and fro of rational knowledge.

I have always been fascinated to imagine the uncertain circumstance in which our ancestors – still barely different from animals, the language that allowed them to communicate with one another just recently born – in caves, around fires, on nights seething with the menace of lightning bolts, thunder claps, and growling beasts, began to invent and tell stories. That was the crucial moment in our destiny, because in those circles of primitive beings held by the voice and fantasy of the storyteller, civilisation began, the long passage that gradually would humanise us and lead us to invent the autonomous individual, then disengage him from the tribe, devise science, the arts, law, freedom, and to scrutinise the innermost recesses of nature, the human body, space, and travel to the stars. Those tales, fables, myths, legends that resounded for the first time like new music before listeners intimidated by the mysteries and perils of a world where everything was unknown and dangerous, must have been a cool bath, a quiet pool for those spirits always on the alert, for whom existing meant barely eating, taking shelter from the elements, killing and fornicating. From the time they began to dream collectively, to share their dreams, instigated by storytellers, they ceased to be tied to the treadmill of survival, a vortex of brutalising tasks, and their life became dream, pleasure, fantasy and a revolutionary plan: to break out of confinement and change and improve, a struggle to appease the desires and ambitions that stirred imagined lives in them and the curiosity to clear away the mysteries that filled their surroundings.

This never-interrupted process was enriched when writing was born and stories, in addition to being heard, could be read, achieving the permanence literature confers on them. That is why this must be repeated incessantly until new generations are convinced of it: fiction is more than an entertainment, more than an intellectual exercise that sharpens one's sensibility and awakens a critical spirit. It is an absolute necessity so that civilisation continues to exist, renewing and preserving in us the best of what is human. So that we do not retreat into the savagery of isolation and life is not reduced to the pragmatism of specialists who see things profoundly but ignore what surrounds, precedes, and continues those things. So that we do not move from having the machines we invent serve us to being their servants and slaves. And because a world without literature would be a world without desires or ideals or irreverence, a world of automatons deprived of what makes the human being really human: the capacity to move out of oneself and into another, into others, modelled with the clay of our dreams.

From the cave to the skyscraper, from the club to weapons of mass destruction, from the tautological life of the tribe to the era of globalisation, the fictions of literature have multiplied human experiences, preventing us from succumbing to lethargy, self- absorption, resignation. Nothing has sown so much disquiet, so disturbed our imagination and our desires as the life of lies we add, thanks to literature, to the one we have, so we can be protagonists in the great adventures, the great passions real life will never give us. The lies of literature become truths through us, the readers transformed, infected with longings and, through the fault of fiction, permanently questioning a mediocre reality. Sorcery, when literature offers us the hope of having what we do not have, being what we are not, acceding to that impossible existence where like pagan gods we feel mortal and eternal at the same time, that introduces into our spirits non- conformity and rebellion, which are behind all the heroic deeds that have contributed to the reduction of violence in human relationships. Reducing violence, not ending it. Because ours will always be, fortunately, an unfinished story. That is why we have to continue dreaming, reading, and writing, the most effective way we have found to alleviate our mortal condition, to defeat the corrosion of time, and to transform the impossible into possibility.

Translated by Edith Grossman.

Portrait photo of Mr. Vargas Llosa by photographer Ulla Montan.